Tales from the Creel

by Rudy Senarighi

All quotations used at chapter headings remain the intellectual property of their respective originators. The author does not assert any claim of copyright for individual quotations. By quoting others, the author does not in any way mean to imply their endorsement or approval of this book or its content.

To the best of the author's knowledge, all quotations used at the beginnings of chapters fall under the fair use or public domain guidelines of copyright law in the United States.

Copyright © 2010 by Rudy Senarighi
ISBN 978-0-615-41029-6
Sturgeon Bay, Wisconsin 54235

PRINTING HISTORY

First edition published October, 2010

Dedication

This book is lovingly dedicated:

First to my family, your support and encouragement prompted me to complete my first book and help sustain my writing.

Second to my two fishing partners Neal and his son Ryan, thank you for sharing our time and adventures in the Arrowhead.

Third to my good friend Andy, you've heard the Whitethroat's call.

Table of Contents

Acknowledgements

My deepest thanks and gratitude:

To Francha Barnard for the help in editing my work, your comments and grammatical expertise has been invaluable.

To Lynn Wiemann for the hours of reading my works and offering help and your perspective, your understanding and ideas helped round out my writing.

To Gina Senarighi for the fine-toothed comb approach you applied my book. Your work, excitement and discussions with me helped put the polish on this work.

To Rachael Ludwig for your beautiful, intricate and inspired illustrations, you went the extra mile to put together such fine drawings.

To all of you, for encouragement, inspiration, sharing your perspectives and insights, your critiques and counsel.

Testament of a Fisherman

I fish because I love to; because I love the environs where trout are found, which are invariably beautiful, and hate the environs where crowds of people are found, which are invariably ugly; because of all the television commercials, cocktail parties, and assorted social posturing I thus escape; because, in a world where most people seem to spend their lives doing things they hate, my fishing is at once an endless source of delight and an act of small rebellion; because trout do not lie or cheat and cannot be bought or bribed or impressed by power, but respond only to quietude and humility and endless patience; because I suspect that we are going along this way for the last time, and I for one don't want to waste the trip; because mercifully there are no telephones on trout waters; because only in the woods can I find solitude without loneliness; because bourbon out of an old tin cup always tastes better out there; because maybe one day I will catch a mermaid; and, finally, not because I regard fishing as being so terribly important but because I suspect that so many of the other concerns of men are equally unimportant - and not nearly so much fun.

-John Voelker (Robert Traver)

PREFACE

"I haven't a clue as to how my story will end. But that's all right. When you set out on a journey and night covers the road, you don't conclude the road has vanished. And how else could we discover the stars?" ~ Author Unknown

A book of my stories had been an idea of mine for years but I was never compelled to actually put pen to paper. Thus, my stories remained just thoughts and a book continued to be only a contemplation of mine. However, serious personal health concerns in February of 2000 acted as a catalyst for becoming actively involved in writing. I began my manuscript late that spring.

Stories are ways in which we pass down information from one generation to another. Over my lifetime I had shared bits and pieces of these tales verbally but had never connected all the parts into a chronicle. Taking the time to record them seems to be the most difficult part of the process. Many times people wait too long to share their tales and the stories are lost forever.

With that big step the writing helped me to put my tales in order.

When I did begin to put my first book to paper, I had no thoughts of ever writing other volumes. That first book was to be a pet project I would complete and have for my daughters, wife and a few close friends.

All people have stories, and most of them contain lessons to be learned or remembered. In penning my first volume, I discovered that there were underlying messages in the tales that I told. However, one common thread throughout my writing is this: Life is not about the end, it is about now. If you focus only on the destination you will miss important things along the way. Take the time to look, see and enjoy the journey.

Those who read my first book commented that the stories brought memories to life for them. Some said the tales helped them understand their inner selves a bit better. Many asked if and when a second book would be written. But a second volume had not been a consideration of mine since I felt all my stories had been told. However, sometimes in reflective moments I would recall events that I had missed while compiling the first manuscript and slowly I began to piece together another series of stories.

Will there be a fourth installment? I know that for me writing cannot be forced. Just as now there may be moments in my future when something will trigger for me an old memory. If enough of those moments occur, there may just be another volume.

Tales from the Creel

Scanlon Creek

"I sat there and forgot and forgot, until what remained was the river that went by and I who watched. On the river the heat mirages danced with each other and then they danced through each other and then they joined hands and danced around each other. Eventually the watcher joined the river, and there was only one of us. I believe it was the river."
~ Norman Maclean (*"A River Runs through It"*)

I have fished many streams during my life. Even though they all hold in common that they are the means by which some nearby spring or wetland drains, each water system has its own unique characteristics. It may be the course that it chooses to cut through the landscape, it could be the color or clarity of the water or the way the water sings as it dances over the bottom. They all have a certain, specific captivating personality.

I also have read about many of the legendary brook trout streams that exist in places just beyond my reach. Many times I fantasized about fishing on the George River in Labrador and daydreamed of hooking into the new world record trout on the Nipigon. But I settled for the fish I imagined from those places, and I am almost certain they are larger and more beautiful than any I could coax from those magical waters in life.

Still, of all the waters that I have plied for trout, the one that I keep going back to in my memory is a small trickle named Scanlon Creek. The exact date or time that I was introduced to the magic of Scanlon Creek are no longer clear to me. I know it was early summer because I can remember the willow tree that we fished under having leafed-out, and a local talking about the wild berry crop.

As I look back on those days, it seems as if my relationship with that stream was always a part of my life. It was the first trout water that I had been introduced to. I had fished on lakes with my father; I even spent a day on the St. Louis River fishing with my uncles, but trout fishing was something new to me.

Scanlon Creek doesn't appear on most topographic maps. It's a small stream, not much more than two miles in length, if it is even that. In comparison to the many rivers I have fished, it is only a tiny trickle, barely two feet wide in some places. On that creek however, my friend, Arvo, introduced me to a new thread in life's tapestry that would continue to weave its way throughout my days.

The creek begins in a marsh area that lies to the west of the small village of Scanlon, Minnesota. I never ventured back into the forest to find its origin, although Arvo and I both were sure that there was a deep, cold, crystal clear pool there. And in the depths of that body of water lurked enormous trout. But that remained a thing of mystery and myth to us. In our minds and tales the pool grew deeper and the trout grew bigger. I'm glad we never found that mystical place. Experiencing it in our fantasies made it the place I wanted it to be and I can go back there any time I wish.

Scanlon Creek drains to the east from the marsh near the small settlement and then flows through a low area between two gravel hills left behind by one of the glaciers that visited the area. After a short, fairly straight and flat run, the creek empties into the St. Louis River.

There wasn't much natural structure in the stream for trout to use for cover. Some places did have undercut banks like the willow tree hole, and there was a log and rock in one stretch, but other than that, some truck tires, and a couple old metal drums provided the only cover for the fish. The willow tree was where Arvo introduced me to some of the secrets of trout fishing.

However, it was purely by chance that we decided to fish that day. Arvo and I, along with most of our friends, had been involved in a project for a week that summer. It was rumored a black bear had been seen a few blocks from my house. A neighbor had been picking berries along the rock outcroppings near the St. Louis River just below Kelly Avenue and said the bear didn't bother him, but he wanted folks to know that one was around. From the location he described, Arvo and I figured the bear must be near one of the places that we neighborhood children used as a "fort" in the woods. Arv and I decided that we should all get together and rid the forest of this menacing creature.

Arv and I began to scrutinize all of the old issues of *Field and Stream* and *Outdoor Life* that we had, looking for a solution to the bear situation. In an article about survival, we found the diagram for a deadfall and decided that this was what we would use. It looked very simple to build, and we thought we could easily get all the materials we needed. If we could get a large enough log for our deadfall, it would kill the bear instantly. Although where and how we would procure a log of the size we needed, then get it to the site of our intended ambush could be an issue, it wasn't important enough to discuss in our initial planning. We figured we would get rid of the bear easily and end up with the makings for a bear rug.

Arv and I started drawing up plans and diagrams for the contraption. We spread the word throughout our neighborhood and soon had enlisted the aid of Scummy, Deepsea, Toodles and Pukkie, all neighborhood chums. Meeting on a street corner with a group of kids that size didn't work, so our group moved into Pukkie's garage to finalize a plan. Unfortunately, with so many great minds working on the project, it soon began to fall apart.

"I think we need to bait the trap."

"Naw, just put it along the trail. He'll walk right into it."

"What if the trap doesn't work? What if it just hurts him?"

"Yeah, he'd be plenty mad."

"Naw, the log will knock him out. We'll make some spears to take along and we can use them to finish him off."

"How are we going to get him out of the woods? He probably weighs 1000 pounds."

"We'll cut him in pieces."

"No, that'll ruin the rug."

"I'll bet my mom could sew the pieces back together."

"That's stupid. We'll ask some of the big guys to come and drag him out with one of their cars."

"No, then they'll want the rug!!"

"My dad says I can't go down there until after the bear is gone."

In the end there was plenty of discussion but a minimal amount of work that happened. The discourse went on for four straight days and slowly interest seemed to wane. Baseball, bike riding and other pursuits pulled the others away until only Arv and I remained and Pukkie's father wanted us out of his garage.

Arv and I collected our things and started to walk back toward his house.

"I don't think the two of us can get that bear," I said to Arv.

"Yeah," he answered, "and besides, I'll bet he's long gone by now anyway. You wanna go fishing?"

I was stunned. I would love to go fishing.

"Sure, but who can drive us to the lake?"

"We don't need a ride. We can bike to Scanlon Creek," he said. "There's lots of trout in that stream."

"Trout? I've never fished for trout."

"It's tricky," Arv said with a smug know-it-all look, "but I'll try to teach you. Get your pole and meet me at my house. We'll dig some worms in my parents' garden."

I stuffed everything I had been carrying into Arvo's arms and pockets then turned to race back to my house. I exploded through the door out of breath and gasped to my mother, "Can I go fishing with Arv?"

She turned from her task at the kitchen counter and, after surveying me and the door I had left open said, "Were you born in a barn? Close that door! You'll let all the flies in."

I instantly realized that she was asking a rhetorical question, so rather than answer it; I promptly complied with her request. Swiftly I walked back to the door, gently closed it and then turned and repeated my question, "Can I go fishing with Arv?"

"Who's is taking you two?"

"No one, we're going alone."

She turned and eyed me up and down. "Where would you be going?"

"Scanlon Creek," I blurted. "We're riding our bikes."

"That little puddle in Scanlon? There aren't any fish in there. That's just a ditch."

"No, no, really. Arv says there are trout in there. He goes there all the time. Please?" I asked. It was more of a request than begging; I was very careful not to put a whiney tone in my voice. That tone was a killer for any requests in my household.

"Okay, you can go. Be home by supper."

"Thanks, ma," I yelled over my shoulder as I bolted out the door.

My trusty fishing pole was in the garage, hung up on the pole holder my father had created out of clothes pins and a piece of pine. The holder wasn't much to look at, but it served the purpose, holding my dad's poles along with my Zebco 66.

I retrieved my pole and broke it down into its two pieces making it much easier to transport across the handlebars of my bike. Next I located my father's tackle box and liberated a package of hooks and split shot sinkers which I tucked into my pants pocket. A quick search in our garbage yielded a nice empty soup can, just right to hold some worms. Feeling adequately supplied for my expedition, I mounted my bike and pedaled up the hill, past Bodie's Grocery Store and half a block on to Arv's house.

I arrived just as Arv came around the back corner of his garage. He was carrying a coffee can that he had filled with dirt and earthworms from his parent's garden.

"Put some of these in your can," he said thrusting the coffee can toward me. "I'll grab my stuff and let's go." With that he headed for the interior of his garage.

In a matter of moments I divided the worm captives into the two cans. Arv appeared out of the darkness of the garage on his bike and whisked past me with a "follow me" over his shoulder.

I leapt on my steed and pedaled furiously until I caught up with him. He led me through the back streets of Cloquet to the top of the hill in Scanlon. Arv coasted through the stop sign on Washington Avenue and began to rocket down the hill toward what I would discover was Scanlon Creek.

"Watch the corner," I barely heard him yell as he disappeared around a curve half way down the hill.

I followed him at a more cautious pace. When I arrived at the place where the creek crosses the road, Arv was impatiently waiting for me with his rod in hand.

"What took ya?" he said. "Let's get going."

And he started along the bank walking upstream. I didn't realize that trout fishing happened on such a tight time schedule. When I fished with my dad in a lake, from a boat, there was lots of leisure time and we never seemed to be in a hurry. Trout fishing was going to be different, or at least trout fishing with Arv.

Arv led and I followed through waist high grass that grew along the side of the stream. He didn't seem to be in such a hurry anymore; as a matter of fact his pace had slowed considerably.

"Walk softly," he cautioned. "You don't want to spook the fish."

"What?'

"If you step too hard on the ground, the fish feel the vibrations and they'll spook. Also, keep the sun in your face."

"Why?' I asked.

"Because you don't want to throw a shadow in the water. The fish will see the movement and spook too."

Boy, this was beginning to seem like something that was more difficult than I wanted to get involved with. I wanted to fish and have fun. Arv was giving me so many things to remember, how could I concentrate on fish? But, I wanted to catch or at least see a trout, so I followed him on.

Suddenly he stopped. He turned to me and gestured toward a large willow tree that was growing on the bank of the stream very close to the waters edge.

"We take it very slow from here," he said in a whisper. "Follow me and stay low."

With that he crouched down so that the grass was chest high and began to shuffle toward the tree. I did likewise. When we were approximately ten feet from the tree, Arv got down lower and began to crawl. While this seemed somewhat strange to me, I followed suit. What did

I know about trout fishing? Besides, this was getting kinda interesting. It was almost like being a spy or a secret agent.

He crawled with me until we reached the base of the tree. In a barely audible whisper he said, "I'm going to peek through the grass. The trout usually lie along the bank here and use the willow roots for cover. If they're here, we'll drop a worm down to them."

Gap-mouthed, I nodded in silence.

Arv gradually parted the grass in front of him and ever so slowly slid his head out of our concealment and over the surface of the stream. He paused for a moment then bit by bit retracted his head back into the grass.

"They're there."

"Let me see,"

"No," he whispered harshly. "You'll spook them. Let's bait up and drop them a worm."

"How do we do that without being seen?"

"We just slide the tips of our poles through the grass, then when they are over the water, let out slack. When you feel a tug, count to five and set the hook."

While we kneeled on the bank, we both baited our hooks. Then in slow unison, we slid our poles through the concealing grass and let our bait drop gently into the waters of Scanlon Creek. The results were almost instantaneous. Both rod tips throbbed slightly, we counted to five, then as one, set our hooks.

Arv's fish made a quick run under the willow tree, became tangled in the roots and broke free. Mine, however, decided to make a run for open water and took off down stream. I stood up and followed it and after a short battle, beached my treasure.

I stood there looking at that fish in awestruck wonder. I had never seen a real brook trout before, only pictures in magazines. The fish lying on the grass before me was beautiful. It looked like it belonged in a tropical aquarium.

Its back was an olive-green, with squiggly lines. The sides were a silvery color and had red spots. But the most striking feature was the fins. They were a pinkish color and had a thin black line with a brilliant white border.

By now Arv had retrieved what he could of his fishing line from the tangle in the willow roots. He came up and stood next to me as I admired my catch.

"Wow. A seven-incher!" Way to go!" He exclaimed excitedly.

I was used to catching fish with my dad in the one to two pound range. Arv was excited over a fish of a few ounces and seven inches long.

"Is he a keeper?" I asked.

"You bet! Six to seven inches is a nice trout. I caught a big one that went ten inches once," he answered. "But those lunkers are pretty scarce."

Looking down at the trout, I was changed. We had stalked our prey, just like the big game hunters did, and I had scored a trophy. I was hooked on trout fishing.

We fished the remainder of the day, but I didn't catch another trout. Arv caught a few, but he seemed to know exactly where they hid and how to get his bait to them. I spent some time watching him and trying to learn what to do. We left the stream with enough time to get home by supper.

I burst into my house and excitedly showed my parents my catch. My mother took me out to the driveway to photograph me and my catch. Although the picture has been lost through the years the memory has not.

A bit later I was enjoying my first trout for supper. Arv had told me the way you cleaned and cooked them included keeping their heads. "Keeps in the sweetness," he explained. My mother didn't agree. "I can't stand the way it looks at me," she said.

He and I spent many days fishing the waters of that little stream during our youth. We each wore out the tips of our rods one season and had to replace them. But as we got older and more mobile, we drifted away from those little waters and began fishing the larger streams. As time went by, the days on Scanlon Creek became just memories but what glorious memories they are.

I am tempted to revisit that little creek again, but have decided against seeing it with adult eyes. I know what it was to me once, a great and mystical waterway that began my journey. I want to remember it through the eyes of my childhood wonder. It is the place where I joined the river.

Heartbreak Canoe

It is not by muscle, speed or physical dexterity that great things are achieved, but by reflection, force of character, and judgment; in these qualities old age is usually not only not poorer, but is even richer. ~ Cicero

"You know, we're not getting any younger," Neal said as he wiped the sweat from his dripping brow. He and I were at the end of the last day of our annual fall trip to Minnesota's Arrowhead. That late September day was cool and beautiful with a cloudless blue sky and not a bit of a breeze. I think there is a special hue of a September sky. It may be the extreme contrast that the fall colors have against the blue sky. The soft greens of spring and the deep greens of summer are gone. The trees are beginning to show their fall glory and even the greens that are left are dull in comparison.

But it was impossible to enjoy the beauty nature provided as we struggled to get our canoe out to our vehicle. The two of us sat in a patch of tag alder taking a break from humping our vessel back to the truck from the stream. This year's growth of the surrounding vegetation presented an incredible tangled barrier for anyone carrying a canoe. As a matter of fact, just walking through it was an ordeal.

On our last trip the previous year we had marked our route in to the stream with surveyors' tape. But the weather and animals had taken their toll on the markers, and we had to pick our way slowly without a trail. We were still a mile from where we had left the truck on the old logging road.

"I know," I answered between gasps for air. "But if the fishing wasn't so fantastic, I would never think of doing this."

Neal and I were on our way back out of Heartbreak Creek, a place we had happened to find eight years earlier due to a chance encounter on a logging road. That day, while making our way into a new stretch of water along an old road, we met a couple of elderly fishermen on their way to a stream we didn't know existed. The conversation that ensued among the four of us was filled with the kind of half-truths and cryptic references that only a trout fisherman could decipher. However, the result of that conversation and some map study on our own, had paid off with the discovery of a remote section of Heartbreak Creek.

That stream had since become a regular stop on our annual trip to the area. We never saw any sign of human access to the stream when we got there and we made sure that we never left any signs when we departed. To this day, I am certain no one other than Neal, his son Ryan, myself and those two old codgers we met on the road ever visit that section of the stream.

In the beginning, the trail into the access point was passable for a four-wheel drive vehicle. But over the years the brush had slowly reclaimed the right of way. We were hesitant to clear any of the new growth from the old road since that would have given anybody a way into our pristine spot. So each year we returned to find that we couldn't drive as far into the creek as the previous year and would have to walk a bit farther. Walking wasn't a problem; however the since animals had taken over using the old roadway as a thoroughfare. That kept a narrow pathway open. But, carrying a canoe in and out through the brush had begun to wear on us.

The exertion of bush-wacking an eighteen foot aluminum canoe through tag alder seemed especially noticeable on this particular September day. On past trips we had stopped for a breather or two and then continued our trek back to the truck. But today both of us seemed to be on the edge of exhaustion and the trip back to our vehicle became an ordeal.

We would trudge ahead a few yards carrying and dragging the canoe and then stop to let our breathing and heart rate slowly return to normal. Neal and I repeated that process for half an hour until we reached the truck.

"Boy, I wonder how many of these trips we have left in us?" I commented. It was a rhetorical statement, but Neal answered it any way.

"A few more, I guess. But I don't think we can continue to bring a canoe in with us. That brush is just getting too thick, and it's taking a bit more out of us than it did twenty years ago. When RF isn't here, we really have to work at this." Ryan, or RF, Neil's son, usually took the lead and did a lot of the heavy work to get the canoe in.

"It's a tough stretch to fish from the shoreline. We could try walking the bank, but we'd miss lots of the best holes. Wading the stream is out of the question. Some of those spots are too deep to get through."

"Yeah . And the road in to here is growing over, too. In a couple of years we'll have to walk all the way in. I really don't want to carry a canoe for a mile and a half," Neal added.

"I agree. We're supposed to get smarter as we get older. We've got to think this thing through and figure a way we can get that canoe in there when Ryan isn't along."

It was a sad moment for us as we silently hoisted the canoe to the top of the truck. While neither of us spoke, we were both thinking the same thing. This may be the last trip into our favorite stretch of trout stream. It would be a bitter pill to swallow, but perhaps the reality of us getting older and nature reclaiming the roadway was something we'd have to accept. Neal and I lashed the canoe to the carriers, loaded the remaining gear into the back of the pickup, then began our slow drive out to the main forest road.

It was getting to be late afternoon, so we made our way back to Crooked Lake Resort, our base of operations. That evening as we packed up for the trip back to our homes, Neal and I talked about Heartbreak.

"Boy, I sure don't want to stop going in there," Neal said. "We got to figure out a way to keep getting into that place."

"Well, maybe we should look at 'ratcheting back' our trip just a bit. If we set a whole day aside just for doing that stream, rather than trying to hit several places in one day, maybe then we could do it. I mean we get up at dawn, eat, pack a lunch and hit the first stream by nine and don't get back to the cabin until close to dark."

"There's still the canoe," he reminded me. "Unless we could get someone to air-drop it in and out, we still have to deal with lugging that thing both ways. It would be nice if we had one in there like Doiv did in the old days"

He was right. The real issue was hauling a canoe that distance. Going in, we were somewhat fresh, but we still expended a lot of energy carrying the 85 pound craft, along with its paddles, cushions and the remainder of our gear. Coming back out after a day of being in the elements and fishing, we were tired if not completely spent. Actually, to use a local term, we were fried. If the day ended right there we would be able to handle it but it didn't. Once we landed at our take-out place on the stream, we would still have a half mile to haul the canoe through some tough tag alder. If the logging road became impassible in the future, we would have a mile and a half to transport it.

To save time with clean-up chores, it was our usual procedure to not cook at our cabin on the last night of the trip. Instead, we traditionally walked up to the Trestle Inn for our supper and a beer or two. This night, the Trestle was serving all-you-can- eat ribs which was one of our favorites. We were looking forward to stuffing ourselves with the special and washing it down with a couple of beers before heading back to our cabin for the night.

The universe works in mysterious ways. There are chance encounters that change your life which can be missed if a person is seconds late or early to a specific place. Years ago we had connected with the two old fishermen on the road to Heartbreak. If we had happened along minutes earlier or minutes later, we never would have met up with them. But, because we were in the right place at that exact moment, we gained access to some of the most unspoiled trout waters that I have ever encountered. A similar thing happened the night we decided to have all-you-can eat ribs. This night we met Pete and a solution to our canoe problem was devised.

The Trestle Inn is never what would be called busy on those late September evenings. There are always a few people in the place, either sitting at the bar with a beer while they watch the TV or at a table enjoying something to eat. Tonight there was a couple at a small table in the corner of the room near the stairway that led downstairs to restrooms that actually had flush toilets

Other than the couple, the only customer in the place was an older man sitting at the bar with a half-finished glass of beer in front of him that he cradled with both hands. The guy wore a tattered flannel shirt with sleeves rolled up to his elbows. From the sweat stains and faded color which adorned it, that garment had seen lots of outdoor use. A knit hat with the remains of a Husqvarna emblem sat at an angle on his head.

The talking stopped and all heads in the tavern/café turned toward the sound of the opening door as Neal and I walked in. We received the customary greeting awarded outsiders entering any small town eatery—a brief noncommittal stare, then just shirt backs as heads swiveled back to their table or to face the mirror behind the bar. The low hum of conversation resumed.

Neal and I took a seat at a table near the bar where we could see the TV screen and soon were approached by the burly waiter/ bartender.

The television reception at the Trestle Inn was weak, and there were only three channels that the antenna could bring in. The selection playing that night was a rerun of an old sit-com. The elderly man at the bar seemed to be riveted to it.

The maître d' took our order and walked toward the bar to get our drinks. Our eyes followed his progress to the two old tap handles that jutted out of the back of the bar. As the glasses slowly filled, the old man began to talk over his shoulder to no one in particular. The barkeep ignored the comment and continued to focus on the tap as it slowly issued forth beer. Neal, the bartender, and I were the only ones near him so I assumed he was talking to one of us and thought it only common courtesy to answer the man. Since the guy pouring our beers wasn't doing it and all I was getting from Neal was a blank stare the task fell to me.

The old guy was facing the television when he said, "Boy, they sure don't write 'em like this anymore." He was referring to the program that was playing at the time. I directed an answer back in his direction.

"Yeah, they don't. Those were different times though. I guess that's part of the reason."

I got up to retrieve our drinks and the bartender handed me two pints of beer. As I picked them up, the old guy pivoted on his stool until he was facing down the bar in my direction. He pursed his lips, gave a knowing nod, then drained the remainder of his glass and tapped the empty receptacle on the bar, the universal signal for "fill 'er up". The bartender responded to his signal by taking the empty glass and slowly filling it.

"You guys staying at the resort?" the old guy asked.

"Yeah. Been there for a few days. We're headed home in the morning."

The barkeep walked toward him and set down a full glass of beer on the bar. The guy acknowledged him with a sideways nod of his head, then continued talking in our direction. "Been fishin?" he asked.

"Yeah. This is the end of our annual trip."

"Howdja do? Any walleyes?"

"Nah, we fish the streams while we're here. Usually go after brookies."

"Where abouts you fishin'?" he inquired.

As I began to walk back to our table I answered in the customary way that trout fisherman do. I didn't give any specific information fearing that I would disclose one of our favorite places to someone who might exploit it.

"We fish north and east of here quite a bit. Sometimes we head back toward Finland or go off the highway toward Murphy City."

"Uh," he grunted as he took a long deep draw on his beer . He set his glass down, then looked at us. He cocked his head to one side, raised one eyebrow and said, "You the guys who been fishing Heartbreak?"

It felt like the air had been sucked out of me. Neal had taken a beer from me and was just starting to drink when the question was asked. His reaction was to purge his nasal passage with most of the brew he had in his mouth. We were both dumbfounded. How could he know about Heartbreak? How could he know that we were fishing that stream?

"Well... uh..." I stammered not knowing how I was going to answer his question and not seem like an outright liar. But it was already too late for that; my pause and stammer must have given me away. Or, it could have been the way Neal sprayed beer from his nose and across the table top. Whatever the cue was, the old guy was on to us.

"Yeah, it's a nice place," he continued. "I seen your truck up there at the old turnoff. I got a place that I stay in at times just down the old road. Must be tough humping that canoe in and out of there, eh?"

As Neal wiped his mouth and mopped up the table I answered that it was quite an ordeal to carry the canoe through the tag alder.

"But, ya know, it's tough to impossible to fish that stretch from the banks. You can't hit the holes from up on top," I added.

"Should leave the canoe in there," he said, and then went back to drinking his beer.

There was an idea that both Neal and I had toyed with on many occasions. We certainly wouldn't be the first to ever do something like that. I thought back to the days when as a younger man I used to fish with John and his father, Doivo.

Doiv had small boats stashed in a few different locations in the Arrowhead and on occasion would guide John and me into one of his places. We would walk through a maze of branches and brush and then suddenly be on the edge of a small stream. While John and I got our poles and gear ready, Doiv would slip off back into the brush. He hardly made a sound as he navigated his way through the intertwined tag alders that canopied us and the creek. We would only sometimes hear a soft splash indicating he had launched his craft into the stream. Most times Doiv and the boat would silently appear out of the thick brush that shrouded the stream and glide to a stop near our feet.

Carrying a boat or canoe in and out of those places each time we wanted to fish them would have really taxed our limits. Not only would the transporting of a craft eat away the time we could be fishing, it would also greatly sap our energy reserves. Having a watercraft already on those streams and available was the ticket. At the end of each trip, Doiv would deposit us on the bank, then paddle off alone downstream to stash his boat.

Hearing about something like that, some people would ask, "Wasn't he afraid someone would steal it?" or "Did he chain it to a tree?" The answer to both of those questions is no. I knew the direction he had gone to hide his boat. I knew the stream we were on and how to find it. Yet, while I could find the stream any time I wanted or walk the direction that Doiv had paddled, I could never find where he hid his boat.

But that was then. Today there are laws about leaving boats unattended or hidden in the woods. The Department of Natural Resources frowns on the practice and has levied some hefty fines on those who do it. So, there are new obstacles to overcome.

I turned to look at Neal who was blissfully smiling and finishing off his pint . (The first one always turns to dust he says.) As he set his empty glass down he commented, "I thought you couldn't just leave boats in the woods. I thought the DNR was against it."

The old guy took a long swig of beer, wiped his mouth with his sleeve and said, "You can leave it on property you own, or at someone's place that you know."

"Yeah, well, the guy that I know who had a place up here is dead. His kid owns it now and it isn't very close to any water. Don't know anybody else."

"My name's Pete. Now you know me," he said. "Leave the damn thing at my place."

"My canoe?"

"Or your boat or your car, I don't care. I'm only about a quarter mile off the water and I cut a trail through to the stream. I'll watch the boat for you, and use it now and again myself. Are ya gonna leave paddles?"

What a stroke of luck! We had stumbled on a place to leave our boat and had not had to surrender any information about our fishing places for it. Over the next hour and several more pints of beer the deal was sealed: we would leave our canoe with Pete. Now we would have a watercraft ready and available to us with an access to the stream we loved to fish and Pete had the use of a boat at any time he wanted.

We got directions to his place and agreed to meet there the next morning on our way back home. We also got directions to his main place of residence in the event that we needed to track him down. Sometimes beer has the effect of making time pass by quickly. Neal and I realized that we had not eaten -the reason we had come to the Trestle in the first place. We knew that food was only served until eight o'clock, so we summoned our bartender and asked about dinner.

"You got a half an hour before we stop serving," he answered.

"We'll have the all-you-can-eat-ribs," we said in unison.

"Okay. But all you can eat right now is one rack each because that's all we have left and we won't be making any more tonight."

For old farts like Neal and me one rack is plenty. To order any more would be an ego trip and a waste of some great food. We ordered, and when the ribs came we ravenously devoured what was before us. There was no conversation only the occasional sucking sounds Neal or I made as we cleaned off a bone. I ate so quickly that I'm fairly certain I didn't taste much of what I ate until later, when it came back around for me, another benefit of old age and eating so late.

Back at our cabin we packed our gear and got ready to head home the next morning as we always do on our last evening. Tomorrow we planned to make a stop on the

Cramer Road. There we would rendezvous with Pete and check out our access point with him.

The next morning Pete showed us his way in. After looking at his entry we set a spring date in early June to come back and hook up with him. Until that time I would be scouring the newspaper ads for an old canoe to leave at Pete's place. After exchanging phone numbers and saying our good-byes, Neal and I were on our way back to Wisconsin.

The seven months until the next meeting seemed to slow down the closer June came. There was an abundance of snow that winter which was good because of the amount of run-off it would provide for fishing but bad because it made the winter drag on. Neal, Ryan, and I phoned and emailed each other up to the first week of June. I procured an old fiberglass canoe for us to leave with Pete. The plan was coming together nicely.

That first fishing trip in June we transported the canoe to Pete's place and used it. I can't describe the good feeling the three of us had when we left that craft at Pete's rather than drag it out through the brush. We used the canoe again in July and on our annual fall trip. It is still there today.

I guess you do get smarter or luckier as you age, and the trout seem to get bigger and more colorful. I was beginning to wonder how many more trips we have left in us. Now the number seems to have been extended indefinitely. There are not many folks left who enjoy crashing through the brush to savor the splendor of nature and the beauty of native brook trout, but Neal and I are among them. If there is an after-life, I know that Doiv is there, looking down on us and smiling

A Boy and His Dog

He wa'n't no common dog, he wa'n't no mongrel; he was a composite. A composite dog is a dog that is made up of all the valuable qualities that's in the dog breed — kind of a syndicate; and a mongrel is made up of all riffraff that's left over. ~ *Mark Twain*

My fishing partner Neal has owned dogs ever since I knew him. They have been of various breeds, but all were well trained, disciplined sporting dogs that he used when he was bird hunting. I hunted over those dogs with Neal and was always impressed by how well they worked.

One fall, Neal offered me an opportunity to hunt pheasants with him and three of his relatives. We would be driving from his cabin in northeast Wisconsin to a game preserve in Michigan to hunt for the day.

"We'll connect with the boys on Saturday morning," Neal told me over the phone. "You and Shirley drive up to the cabin Friday and spend the night. We'll get an early start and be back by mid-afternoon."

That sounded great to me and I quickly agreed.

Shirley and I made the hour long drive Friday evening and arrived at dusk. As we crested the hill just before Neal's place, I could see the soft glow of the gas lights through the windows of the cabin. After many trips to the cabin, the unspoken warm welcome of this sight never fails to move me.

We spent the evening checking and packing our gear in preparation for a smooth start in the morning. There wasn't much of the usual banter that precedes our trips. We turned in early to get plenty of rest for the next day.

As usual, Neal was up with the first light. I heard him rattling pots and pans in the kitchen and soon smelled the heady scent of morning coffee brewing. I knew it would soon be followed by the smell of sausage frying which was the signal breakfast was almost done.

It was warm under the covers and I had to coax myself out. I had the blankets tucked up tightly around my shoulders leaving only my nose exposed. I knew there would be a blast of cool air as soon as I emerged from my cocoon, but it was a small price to pay for the great day ahead.

I rolled out of bed being careful not to wake Shirley. I quickly dressed in the clothes I had laid out the night before and went downstairs. Neal's dog, Rose, a black and white English Pointer, greeted me at the foot of the stairs. She is usually a calm animal, that is, until she senses there may be a hunting excursion in the immediate future. That morning she recognized or smelled the clothing we were wearing and paced nervously between the kitchen and front door whining occasionally.

Finally she stopped and sat at the door. Rose stared intently toward Neal and me, and the slightest indication that either of us was paying any attention in the direction of the door or her would elicit rapid tail wagging and a low whining.

The table was set and a steaming cup of coffee had been poured next to my plate.

"One egg or two?" Neal yelled from the kitchen.

"Feels like a two egg morning," I called back.

He flash-fried four eggs and served them with sausage. We wolfed down the breakfast, cleared the dishes, cleaned up the kitchen and were out the door in roughly fifteen minutes. Rose had raced outside as soon as the door was opened. She sat impatiently near the truck's tailgate. Neal kenneled her in the back of the truck, we did a quick check of the equipment we had packed the evening before and then were on our way to rendezvous with the rest of our hunting party.

The weather that Saturday was perfect for our excursion. The brilliant blue sky was clear of clouds giving a fresh clean feeling to the day. The temperature was a crisp fifty degrees with no wind. The grass in the fields had taken on that golden color of fall. Trees and shrubs were skeletal since the majority of the leaves had fallen or been blown off by earlier breezes.

"These guys we're meeting have a dog, too," Neal said.

"Great," I said. "It will be fun to hunt over two dogs."

"Well," Neal added, "Frank is a little rough."

"Frank?"

"Yeah that's the dog's name. My cousin bought him and wants to hunt him, but he hasn't spent much time training him."

"What?" I said. "How does he expect the dog to hunt?"

"Well, the dog is a retriever and a retriever is a hunting dog, so my cousin figures it just follows that the dog will know how to hunt and retrieve. He also knows that Rose is a great dog and he figures Frank will learn by watching what Rose does."

"Can he control the dog?"

"Well, he does have the dog fitted with a shock collar. But, he uses it so much Frank is beginning to take on the glassy-eyed look of a client from the canine version of *One Flew over the Cuckoo's Nest*."

"So this dog will hunt and retrieve and hone its skills by watching and mimicking what Rose does?"

"That's pretty much it."

I didn't reply, just shook my head. It seems that some people have a misconception about dogs; they believe that dogs have an innate ability to perform certain tasks or that these animals can reason like a human being in English. Some treat their pets as if they were human, scolding them and giving them a time out as a deterrent to unwanted behavior. This exchange with Neal rekindled memories of dogs I have encountered throughout my life and how those beliefs played a part in my experiences.

I grew up watching the adventures of Lassie and Rin-Tin-Tin on a black and white television. Those two dogs embodied what I believed a pet should be. They were always smart, loyal, and brave. Lassie regularly saved little Timmy from some peril and Rin-Tin-Tin rescued Rusty from the jaws of death. "Yo, Rinny" or "Get help, girl" were the only commands needed for those animals spring into action. I had the same longing for a dog that most kids do, but mine was fueled even more by watching the exploits of the two on TV. I envied the affection and dedication that those two creatures shared with their masters and fantasized about the exploits that I would have if I had my own dog.

My parents must have sensed my desire for a pet. They brought a puppy home when I was about five years old. The dog was a beagle and its name was Sparky. My father named the dog after one he had had when he was young. Sparky was energetic and playful as most puppies are as well as being what I thought was incredibly smart. She would come when her name was called almost immediately. I knew, deep in my heart, that the two of us were destined for incredible adventures.

I thought the world of that dog and was certain Sparky felt the same way about me. I was sure she had the same qualities as the two animals whose exploits I followed on TV. I knew Sparky would never let me down and would probably give her life to save me. She was, in my mind, a magnificent animal.

Those thoughts were dashed the day I fell off my tricycle while trying to avoid crashing into my pet. I was racing along the sidewalk in front of our house attempting to outdistance the cars that slowly cruised along our street. Sparky was valiantly trying to keep in front of me as I blazed along, wind in my hair and the streamers on the ends of my handle bars stretched out straight. For some reason known only to her, Sparky abruptly slowed her gait and turned directly in front of me. I quickly twisted my handlebars away from Sparky and tried to avoid hitting her, but tricycles have no brakes. My front wheel hit the edge of the grass that bordered our sidewalk and my conveyance immediately stopped. I, however, did not.

The laws of physics took over. I catapulted out of my seat and over my handle bars, bounced on the blacktop surface of our street and skidded to a stop. As I lay in a crumpled heap at the edge of the road, I tried to catch my breath and evaluate my condition. The palms of my hands, my knees and my chin were scraped and raw. I was sure that I was mortally injured and barely dared to move. I was certain that I needed professional help. Naturally, I called upon my trusty companion to get that help.

"Sparky, girl, get help!" I moaned from my prone position. "Get help girl, Ricky's hurt," I pleaded.

I waited for her to spring into action, just as Lassie or Rinny would do. She would, I knew, sniff me, whine a bit, then bolt for home to summon aid.

However, Sparky took a different approach to my situation than the TV dogs did. She walked over to me wagging her tail, licked my face and then rolled over on her back and lay down next to me on the sidewalk.

It was about that time that a car drove up and slowed down as it neared me. The driver rolled down his window and yelled, "Hey, kid, are you all right?"

I sheepishly answered, "Yeah."

With that, I slowly got up, righted my trike and rode back toward my house with Sparky tagging along behind. What a letdown. At that moment I was not thinking very happy thoughts about my companion.

Sparky stayed with us for the better part of her puppyhood. However, her beagle instincts took over during her juvenile stage. One day while lying on our back porch she caught sight of a rabbit in our backyard. She jumped to her feet and with a series of long, mournful howls, took off after that bunny. That was the last time anyone in our family ever saw Sparky.

My brother was born shortly thereafter and the two of us boys added enough excitement to our family to preclude the need for any other large pet. My brother and I had goldfish, turtles, and a couple of parakeets, but nothing that took as much time and responsibility as a dog. Occasionally as I was growing up I would dream about owning a hunting dog like the ones described in *Field and Stream* or *Outdoor Life*; an animal that hunted, retrieved, and obeyed your every command. None of my childhood friends nor I ever owned such an animal.

As I got older this desire became even deeper, especially during duck hunting season. My buddy Arvo and I would jump shoot (stalk isolated inlets and scare whatever ducks are using that water as a safe harbor) along the St. Louis River. The birds would "jump" into the air to attempt to fly away while we hunters would attempt to shoot them. We were fairly successful with this approach, but it seemed whenever we did hit a duck, it would fall twenty feet from shore. We'd try using branches to reach our quarry or constructing rudimentary walkways out of available brush, but someone always got wet in the attempt.

"God, this water is cold," I said as I waded out to retrieve a downed duck.

"Shoulda wore our hip boots," Arv would yell from the shore. "Or, wait 'til they swing closer to land before we shoot."

"I'd need waders. The water is up to my waist!"

I could never adequately explain to my mother why I came home wet and smelling from the paper mill sludge that covered the bottom of the river.

"How could you get so wet and dirty duck hunting?" She'd ask.

I didn't know it then, but the appropriate response was, "If you need to ask the question, you won't understand the answer."

We did come close to the luxury of canine companionship the year our friend, Jerry, bought a dog. Jerry lived in our neighborhood and was four years older than we were. He had his driver's license and was also a hunter. Arvo and I hung out with him, or rather Jerry allowed us to hang out with him as long as we remained socially subservient.

Being older, Jerry was naturally wiser than we were and demanded the respect that was required of an elder. He was handy with tools and could fix just about anything mechanical. It was exciting to be around him because he seemed to be always tinkering with something or coming up with an exciting plan or project, the results of which were not always received well by the adults in our lives.

Once when Arv and I were eleven years old, Jerry's father told him to use or get rid of a large pile of scrap pieces of wood stored behind their house. I think he ended his directive with something to the effect of, "I don't want to see that pile of crap behind the house when I get home from work tonight." The wood was left over from the multiple endless building projects and renovations that seemed to always be going on at Jerry's house. That day he enlisted the help of Arvo and me to re-pile, sort and discard the assortment of lumber.

In the morning as Jerry's father left for work, the three of us began carrying the wood from the backyard pile to the edge of the street in front of the house. That would make it easier for the junkyard people to cart the lumber away. As we made our trips back and forth between the front and back yards, a plan began to form in Jerry's mind.

"It's too bad we have to throw this stuff away," he said. "If we could get it down to the woods, we could build a great tree house with it."

"Yeah, but it would take forever to carry all this stuff there," Arv answered.

"Wish the woods was closer," I said.

"Wait," Jerry said, "what if we build a tree fort here?"

"In your yard?"

"Yeah, my dad said get rid of it or use it."

"You don't have a tree big enough," I reminded him.

"What if we didn't build it in a tree? What if we built it on the lawn?"

"A fort?" Arvo asked.

"No, a boat, a PT Boat," Jerry said as he became more excited about his plan. "We could make it just like the one Kennedy had in World War Two. We could use it to play war."

"Won't your dad care?" Arv and I both asked.

"Nah, he said use it or get rid of it. We'll have the only yard with a PT Boat in it. We could even charge kids to ride in it."

"You mean we'll float it someplace?"

"No, stupid, we can pretend. We can have the kids get in and then you two can stand outside of it and rock it back and forth. It'll be great," he said excitedly.

When Jerry's father returned home from work that evening, the pile of lumber in the back yard was gone. All that remained of where it had been was a large area of dead grass. However, sitting in the middle of the front lawn was a twenty-five foot long rough replica of a Navy PT boat complete with a ten foot tall mast and bridge.

We thought it was a masterpiece and by the gap-jawed expression on Jerry's father's face, we knew he was duly impressed. It had taken us all day to construct our boat. Under the direction of Jerry's father it took just a few hours that evening to completely dismantle it and pile the remains next to the street. Our vessel's lifespan rivaled the Titanic.

But, the real story here is about the dog Jerry bought one year for the purpose of hunting. Prior to purchasing a hunting dog there are several things to be considered, not the least of which is breed selection. Since this dog would be primarily hunting birds, good choices could be pointers, setters, or retrievers. Jerry, however, purchased a mixed breed Black Lab-German Shepherd. His rationale for this choice was greatly influenced by the dog's seller.

"Lab's a good water dog," The seller said. "And, the German Shepherd was the closest thing to a wolf you can get. Wolves are natural hunters you know."

That and the price of twenty-five dollars was all Jerry had to hear. The deal was struck and he owned a dog. He named the dog Chica, which is supposed to be Spanish for *girl*. As I look back, I remember that Chica was not a girl, and Jerry had no knowledge or connection to anything remotely Spanish, but the name was something special to him. Chica was an overly friendly canine, weighed in at about 100 lbs and was prone to leaping up on a person and slobbering all over them with a tongue much like a warm, wet flannel blanket.

Some people are naturally in tune with their dogs, and by their behavior direct the dog into meeting their expectations. Jerry met the first criteria but fell short on the other. He did spend some time in his yard with Chica trying to teach him to fetch and heel. After about an hour, Jerry was certain that Chica had mastery- level skills. He excitedly told us this duck season we would have "hunting machine" to retrieve for us.

That fall, Arvo, Jerry and I planned meet before dawn to hunt ducks one October Saturday. Jerry had begged his father for the use of his pickup truck.

Deadfish Lake is a small swamp-bordered lake west of our town. The area the lake is in is locally known as Ditch Banks. That region is a large undeveloped lowland area with many small lakes. It provided prime hunting and trapping for anyone who wished to utilize it. There were stories about the region passed down by word of mouth from generation to generation which gave it an aura of mystery; tales of ghost Indian Princesses, packs of hungry carnivorous animals and stretches of bog and quicksand, among a few. As with all the areas we hunted and fished, there were places in the Ditchbanks that were too difficult or remote to readily access.

But Deadfish Lake was in our reach. We could drive within a mile of either end of the lake and walk an old tote road in to the shore. A stream entered the lake on the west side and exited the lake on the east which provided the best places to set up a duck blind. Because the lake was so accessible and such a good spot to duck hunt there were many who attempted to hunt there. If you wanted to get set up in one of those two best places, you needed to get to the lake early.

Jerry's father consented to his plea for the use of the pick-up truck for the day. However, his father salvaged scrap iron for a living and the pick-up was full of scrap from a recent job. It was not going to be unloaded for a hunting trip.

"You and your buds can take the truck," he had told Jerry, "but the scrap stays put. And you better not lose any of it either or you guys pay for the missing stuff."

Jerry agreed. We didn't care. We figured the extra weight would give us more traction on those back roads. It did mean the three of us, Chica and our guns would all have to ride in the cab for the ten mile trip to Deadfish Lake. But being cramped wasn't new to us. Arv and I had crossed the St. Louis River with three dozen decoys in a one-person boat before. If we had put one more shotgun shell in that boat it would have sunk. We figured we were pretty good at utilizing whatever space was available for pack gear.

The three of us made plans to meet at Jerry's house that Saturday morning at four a.m. Sunrise was at 6:30, so we would have plenty of time to drive to the Ditchbanks, walk the road into the lake, and set up before first light. By starting that early we would probably beat anyone else to the lake and be able to secure one of the two best sites for hunting.

I always set an alarm, but I don't remember ever being awakened by one. I was always up before it would go off, my internal clock not allowing me to sleep. That Saturday was like many in October for me. I quietly got out of bed and went into our living room where I had left my hunting clothes and gear the night before. The living room was the furthest room from the bedrooms in our house. I could dress there with a light on without waking anyone. The routine was to quickly dress, gobble down some cereal, jot a quick note reminding my folks where we would be hunting and hurry the two blocks to Jerry's house.

I remember those dark, cold October mornings of my youth in Minnesota vividly. The cool dampness would smack you in the face as you exited the house, sucking the warmth off of your exposed skin. It wasn't the biting cold that winter brings, but it did send a quick chill through you. If the sky was clear, the stars sparkled like ice crystals or the moon cast long shadows across the landscape. It was a time of almost utter silence and peace, the only sound being the wind or a distant whistle from the paper company.

When I arrived, Arvo was standing in Jerry's driveway. There was a slight cloud of vapor around his head, the remnants of his breath as he exhaled. He shifted from foot to foot as he did the customary dance hunters and fisherman do on cold mornings in an attempt to keep warm.

The door to the house opened as I approached and Chica burst out of the house ahead of Jerry. He was wagging his tail furiously while running circles around Arv and me. He stopped at each of us long enough to jump up toward our faces and slap us head-on with his enormous, wet tongue.

"God!!! Call this idiot off will ya?" Arv yelled. He had never been a true admirer of the dog.

Jerry walked over to the dog, grabbed a fist full of hair on the scruff of his neck and dragged the animal toward the truck. He opened the truck's cab door and briskly ushered Chica inside.

"Let's go," he said, "we'll be burning daylight soon." Jerry liked that phrase and had taken to using it since he'd heard it in a western movie.

We crammed ourselves and our gear into the truck and began our expedition to Dead Fish Lake. As I look back, the trip now seems akin to the performance of one of those clown cars that used to appear at a circus; the one where a small car stops in the center of the middle ring, the doors suddenly burst open and fifteen or twenty clowns pour out of the vehicle. People are amazed at how many bodies could be stuffed into such a small car.

The interior of the truck was similar to what the inside of one of those clown cars must have been. Jerry, Arv, myself, Chica, three shotguns, two dozen duck decoys, hip boots and ammunition were stuffed into every nook and cranny. Our situation was a bit different because Chica couldn't decide just where he was going to stay. He would lie on the floor, then try to get up and turn around, then attempt to push his way up and get on our lap or try to stick his head out the side window. This activity was very annoying to Arv and me and affected Jerry's driving somewhat. We did eventually arrive at the old road access to Dead Fish no worse for the wear and attempted to begin our hunt.

Things began to look dim as soon as the truck doors opened. Before any of the three of us could exit, Chica rocketed out of the truck and was engulfed by the early morning darkness. This presented a problem since Chica was black in color and therefore more than difficult to see.

Jerry became nervous and started yelling for his dog, but Chica was not disciplined enough to return when his name was called. This was due to an oversight in the training regime Jerry had followed; he assumed that Chica knew his name and, of course, would return whenever called.

"We can't walk into the lake without him," Jerry wailed. "He doesn't know where we're going. He'll get lost out here alone!"

"He'll come back to the truck after he's run around some," I said. "Let's get moving, it's going to be light before we get into the lake if we don't."

"But, if he comes back and we're not here, he won't know what to do."

"Leave him a note and the truck keys," Arv said sarcastically, and with that he began to head down the road toward the lake. I fell in behind Arv and was followed quickly by Jerry.

Sounds seem amplified in the darkness. A chipmunk running through the brush sounds enormous. We had not walked far down the road into the inky darkness when we heard what sounded like a stampede of cattle coming toward us. The hoof beats kept coming closer and we could not see what was making the sound. When it sounded like the animal was right in front of us the noise stopped and so did we. Almost immediately Arv let out a high-pitched scream.

"It's on me!!! Help!!!"

Then in a bit less of a frantic tone, "Oh, God!! Get this idiot off of me!!"

Chica had found us. He had run full speed in the dark toward us, and when he was within range had launched himself, in the darkness, at the nearest person to express his joy in being back with the group. Unfortunately he had picked the lease enthusiastic Chica fan among us. That was the first time on this trip that Arv wanted to shoot Chica. After some pleading by Jerry to spare his pet's life, we were on our way again into the lake.

The rest of the trip slowly deteriorated into a comedy of errors, all of which began to erode any positive feelings Arv or I had about this dog. Chica would lie quietly in our duck blind then suddenly decide to burst from the grass and swim among our decoys. That had a less than positive effect on attracting any ducks into our area. Jerry tried to remedy this by holding Chica down or tying the dog to his belt with a short piece of rope. This resulted in Jerry either being jerked off his feet when the dog made a rush for the water, or continuous long howls and wails from Chica.

We tried to ignore the dog's behavior until just about noon that day. The ducks had chosen to use the far end of the lake all that morning; none flew anywhere close to us.

"I've had it," Arv said. "we're wasting a day here. The ducks are not going to come close with that hound acting like he is. Let's pack it up."

"Yeah," I agreed. "We can hit some puddles on the way home and maybe jump shoot some."

Jerry concurred. We were standing up when Arv hissed, "Get down. Here comes one."

We looked over the top of the blind and couldn't believe it. Coming straight into our decoys, with her wings set, was a large hen mallard.

"Arv, you take her," Jerry said. I think he was trying to placate Arv for the miserable day he'd endured so far.

We all waited for the duck to get into range. When she had entered our airspace, Arv stood up, aimed and fired. The hen crumpled in midair, then splashed down into the middle of our decoys, dead.

"All right! Nice shot," I said to him.

"Yeah, but does that dog retrieve?" Arv asked as he slowly lowered his shotgun.

"Of course!" Jerry snapped back, annoyed that anyone could doubt the skills of his dog.

Jerry dragged Chica by the scruff of his neck to the edge of the water. He then reached in his pocket and pulled out a handful of rocks.

"What are you doing?" Arv asked.

"I need to show him where the duck is," was Jerry's answer. "I'll throw a couple of rocks out there and then Chica will swim out and get your duck."

Arv let out a barely audible groan.

"What next?" he said under his breath.

Jerry threw the rocks. Chica swam to the splash; he grabbed Arv's duck, swam back to shore with it, then ran past us into the tall grass and began to eat the duck. When Jerry approached the dog, Chica snarled and bared his fangs. Arv threatened to shoot Chica for a second time. However, this threat had a bit more teeth in it than the first one; he now had a loaded shotgun.

There was a lot of shouting and yelling. Jerry convinced Chica to give up the remains of the duck by utilizing a piece of driftwood he found as an attention-getter. Once Jerry had Chica's attention, he easily extracted the remnants of the mallard from the mix. Arv didn't shoot the dog and did get half a duck breast to take home. Even so, it was clear this was the last straw for him. I acted as a buffer and walked between them all the way back to the truck. Our day of hunting was over.

Though Jerry, Arv and I went on many more hunting trips together, Chica never accompanied us again. As a matter of fact, I never again hunted with an animal that was as noncompliant as Chica; that is, until I met Frank.

"So, Frank is going to learn to be a hunting dog by watching Rose?" I asked Neal.

"Yeah, that's pretty much it."

"Did I ever tell you about the time Jerry's hunting dog ate our duck?"

Scott Creek and Other Lies

"It's not their fault that they lie, they're fishermen."
~Kurt Schumacher, Crooked Lake Resort

There wasn't a cloud in the sky to block the intense rays of the sun. We were accustomed to cool weather when we fished in the spring but this day was more like a day in mid July. A breeze would have helped some, but there was not a breath of air moving. Deer flies were making strafing runs at our heads as we worked our way through the tag alders. The only thing that kept them from landing very often was the sweat streaming off of us. The insects would dive bomb with the velocity of a rifle bullet but were unable to gain a purchase with their feet when they hit. Their attempts at getting an easy lunch were much like kids using a "Slip and Slide" on a hot summer day.

As we paused to take our bearings and to help stay the rivulets of perspiration, Neal said, "There's got to be an easier way into this place." I can't remember how many times we have made that statement.

"If that were true," I answered, "I think we'd see a lot of fresh sign in here. Broken branches, trash or tracks maybe, but we've only seen an old can or two and those have been here for quite a while. My dad used to say nothing worthwhile is ever easy."

"Yeah, and sometimes half the fun is just being there. I've heard that all before," Neal answered as a large drop of sweat dripped from the end of his nose and splattered on the toe of his boot.

Neal or I have had this same conversation a thousand times over our years of fishing and tramping through the brush in the Arrowhead. It usually occurred as the two of us paused from bushwhacking our way into a secluded stretch of water. The sequence of events normally was; choosing a stream that someone had mentioned, locating a place where the flow looked to be close to a road or trail of some sort, driving or walking to that spot, taking a compass bearing from that point, breaking down our poles for easier carrying, then heading off in the direction the stream should be. No matter how closely we would estimate the distance to be or the amount of time it should take to walk to the stream bank, time and distance always seemed to increase geometrically as we battled our way through the tag alder.

We have studied maps and aerial photographs of numerous streams and lakes, trying to discern a hidden path or byway with which to access them. Sometimes our studies have paid off with the discovery of an abandoned rail line, or the remnants of an old winter road. The majority of the time, however, we have found there is no easy way in. But, before we even get to the point of choosing a place to fish, we need to get some accurate information about the spot; most importantly, the location.

Getting truth from a fisherman is not easy, and getting the whole story from a fisherman is nearly impossible. As a group, they don't give up their secret places to just anyone. An example is this interchange between fishermen and a couple of strangers.

"Did you get those fish in the lakes or stream?"

"We only stream fish."

"Oh wow. Were you fishing the Baptism?"

"I'd tell ya, but then I'd have to kill ya."

You need to become a trusted member of their elite group of individuals, which takes time and in some cases, an initiation process or some demonstration of your worthiness. But, even in the tallest tales there is a hidden grain of truth. Part of being a fisherman is the ability to ferret out those small grains and try to expand on them. This is the reason Neal and I were sweating our way through the brush on our way into Scott Creek.

Although I had heard of the small stream many years before, the real motivation began one evening in Fred's cabin near Isabella. The gas lights gave out a dim glow inside the cabin as Neal and I relaxed at the old kitchen table. We were at the end of an enjoyable day of fishing and had just sat down to savor two fingers of bourbon before dinner. The cabin was filled with pieces and parts of things; artifacts that had been collected and left there over the past sixty years by hunters and fisherman. There were all sorts of flotsam and jetsam hanging from nails that protruded from the walls or stacked haphazardly on the few rudimentary shelves above the windows. Neal was slowly surveying our surroundings as he sipped his drink.

"Where do you suppose he caught those?" he asked as he stared at the old, discolored mounts that hung on the wall of Fred's cabin. "Those are some big trout."

The time-worn fish had been decorations on the old cabin wall for as long as I had been coming to Isabella. They were a matched set of brook trout, each 21" in length, and judging from their girth, they must have weighed four or five pounds each. Over the years that Fred was alive I had attempted to pry clues out of him about where those fish came from. The most I ever got was that they came out of Scott Creek. Even though Scott Creek was a narrow trickle of a stream, it covered a lot of area. Getting even that shred of information about a fishing spot from him was unusual.

"Fred told me he caught those two back-to-back in Scott Creek," I answered. "It's a narrow little creek, runs through some meadows and almost disappears in places. Fred said these came out of a clearing near an old lumber camp site."

"We've never fished Scott," Neal said. "How come we don't go there?"

"Let me show you something," I said as I got up to get our maps of the area.

I unrolled the Isabella quadrangle on the table that served as a work space and eating area for the cabin.

"Here's where we are," I said indicating the location of Fred's cabin. "And here is Scott Creek."

"It's not that far from here. We could easily drive up and fish that in a morning."

"Just a minute," I added. Pointing to another thin blue line on the map I added "Here is another branch of Scott Creek, and here," I said as I took out two more topographic maps, "is the rest of Scott Creek. We can easily find the creek; what we don't know is where Fred fished it. And, since he is dead, I can't try to get the information out of him."

"Oh, I see. There's a lot of area. But he must have told someone. What about his grandkids? They fished up here a lot."

"My cousins? Well, I can try to weasel it out of them, but they won't give up any information about a good place to fish. You or I certainly wouldn't. But, it's worth a try. They just might slip up."

Our conversation drifted to other things as we finished our bourbon. Then it was on to dinner prep. I sliced the spuds and onions while Neal rinsed the trout that had been delegated to the evening fry pan. When the potatoes and onions were just about done, they were given a blanket of cheddar cheese and put on a low back burner to simmer. I heated olive oil in our large cast iron fry pan, and when the surface began the telltale shimmer that hot oil gets, I dropped the trout in one by one. They were so fresh that I had to hold them in the fry pan as they sizzled. When golden brown and crispy they came out of the pan and rested for a moment, but not too long, on a piece of paper towel. Neal set the table and we sat down to eat our feast as the gas lights sputtered above our heads. Aside from an occasional grunt or sigh, the lights were the only sound during our meal.

We spent the next days fishing some of our favorite places and we kept enough fish for a meal and to take some home. There was some talk between us about how I would approach my relatives and try to pry the Scott Creek information out of them, but I already had hatched a scheme. Now all I had to do was find a time when they were all together and in a comfortable place so I could spring my plan into action. Individually they were very tight-lipped, but in a group there was a chance that some stories would get mixed and information would be leaked.

Getting relatives together was always difficult. At this stage of our lives, the only times that happened were at funerals or weddings. Unfortunately, everyone was healthy and in no imminent danger of dying, so the only hope for a meeting was a nuptial. As fate would have it, that August a niece decided to get married, and the family gathered for the event. The reception seemed to offer the most conducive place to glean information from my clan.

All the male cousins were standing to one side of the bar when I walked into the reception hall. They turned as I entered, acknowledged me with a nod, then went back to their animated discussion while each nursed a bottle of beer.

Ah, I thought, alcohol. This was a tongue-loosener that I hadn't planned on but would try to use to my benefit. My experiences in the past with liquor and fishermen was that, as the night wore on and the beer flowed, the stories got better and better and the chances for a misstatement or two increased.

I got myself a drink then joined the group and engaged in small chit-chat. Talk about our jobs, families, cars, kids and the weather was bantered about. This was all good stuff, nothing that we talked about would raise any suspicion about my motives to extract valuable fishing specifics from them. Our conversation began to wane, and I seized the time to gently change the subject.

"So, you guys ever get back to Fred's place?" I asked nonchalantly.

You could feel the mood of the group change slightly. I perceived a slight tenseness in them.

"Yeah," my cousin Jason answered for the group, "why do you ask?"

"Oh, I was thinking about all the stuff that was in that old cabin is all. There was a lot of old crap in there."

Relaxing a bit he said, "Still is."

"Those two old trout still hanging on the wall?" I asked, pretending not to know.

"Last time I was there," Jason responded as the others stood by silently and just nodded.

"Boy, I was impressed with those when I was kid. How about I get you guys another round while we stand here?" I offered.

They all drained the last dregs from the bottles they were holding and gave me the head bob that signified a yes answer.

"Be right back," I said, and turned to get their beverages.

When I returned, Jason suggested we all grab a chair at a nearby table. "Take a load off and shoot some more bull," he suggested. So that's what we did.

We talked about our childhood together, adventures we had had as kids, and slowly the conversation turned back to the Arrowhead and fishing. It was during the next round of drinks that I broached the subject of those fish again.

"Fred ever say where he caught those two brookies?"

"Yah," Jason responded. "Said they came out of Baptism Crossing. That was one of his favorite places. That's where we dumped his ashes."

Lee, who had been quiet most of this time leaned forward and said, "No. He got those out of the Dumbbell River."

Jason pounced on his statement. "Who told you that?"

"Grandpa did."

"There's no trout in the Dumbbell River."

"Yeah there is!"

"Oh, ever caught any?"

"You betcha! Right where Scott Creek empties into it. There's a big...." His eyes met mine as his answer trailed off.

"Fred mentioned that he liked to fish Scott Creek. Said he took a lot of fish out of there. He said there was a place near an old lumber camp where they could pile logs to float out in the spring."

"That doesn't sound like any place I've heard of," Jason answered as his steely-eyed stare bored into Lee.

The conversation turned to other matters and continued to drone on but I paid little attention to what was discussed. The brief interchange between my two cousins had been enough. I had it! The place where Scott Creek emptied into the Dumbbell River. That had to be Fred's place. Now, I needed to get to a map and find a route to that spot. Once that was done, Neal and I would be able to plan out our spring trip to the Arrowhead and include a day for finding Scott Creek.

That fall passed, filled with bird hunting and some late stream fishing for salmon. Winter set in and offered enough snow to accommodate a few days of snowshoeing before the spring sun began to rot away the ground cover. Neal and I had maintained contact throughout the winter months and had sketched out a plan for the spring. We would spend one day driving up to the Arrowhead. After unpacking, we would use whatever daylight we had left to fish one of the two nearby trout lakes. The next morning we would head for the confluence of Scott Creek and the Dumbbell River and spend the majority of that day plying the waters there.

Our map research revealed a fine, dotted line that connected the two streams to a logging road. That dotted line must be a snowmobile trail or an old road to be indicated on the topo. It should be easy to find. On paper, it looked like we simply needed to drive the logging road in to where the dotted line met the roadway, leave our vehicle and walk a short distance to the water. But it seems that the words "simple" or "easy" can't be used to describe anything to do with this area. In order to get to the prime fishing, you need to work. It's like an artist has to suffer before they become famous.

On the chosen day we drove to the junction of the logging road and the general grade road. General grade is a term that's used to describe the dirt roads that crisscross the forests of northern Minnesota. Most of them can be traversed by car. Logging roads are different story. Most of them do have a good solid base of gravel, but they are usually pock-marked with hidden springs and heavily rutted from years of trucks and logging equipment traffic. Many also are studded with large boulders that jut out of the surface at odd angles and various heights.

We stopped the truck and got out to survey the first few feet of the road. It looked solid and had not been traveled in a long time. There was a rather large, water-filled hole in it that took up about half the width of the road at a particularly narrow point. On one side of the road was a ravine that dropped off about five feet. On the other side was a large boulder that the loggers must have pushed there with a bulldozer. It might even have come out of the large hole in the road itself. If we were to drive on this road, we needed to drive between the boulder and the ravine and go partially through the mudhole.

"Think it's deep?" Neal asked as we stood surveying the obstacle.

"Well, let's find out. Look for a long stick so we can measure the depth."

"This place is picked pretty clean. Looks like the loggers took or burned whatever trimmings there were."

"You know, I didn't notice this before, but there's water running out of that hole and draining down into the ravine. That's not good."

"You think it's a spring?" Neal asked.

"Let's check something. Help me with some rocks."

We gathered a number of small, melon-sized boulders and brought them to the edge of the hole. I threw the first one in and it disappeared from sight.

"I gotcha," Neal said. "We'll build up the bottom of the mudhole with some rocks, then be able to drive right over. Good idea."

It was a good idea, in theory. However, we threw every available rock into that hole only to have each one disappear into the depths. We guessed it was a spring, and it was a deep one. There would be no driving directly through that abyss.

We scrutinized the mud hole, the road width and the terrain. After considerable thought and discussion, we decided that the truck could squeeze through the area between the edge of the mud hole and the edge of the road that bordered the ravine. The worst things that could happen would be a slip over the edge of the ravine, in which case the truck would hang up on its frame, or a slide into the spring and the truck would then bottom out and hang up on its bumper. If either of those happened, it would only mean that we would spend part of the day digging and jacking the truck to get it out, or we would need to walk back out on the general grade road until we saw another vehicle or reached someone's house.

"You watch the front wheels," Neal said to me, "and I'll pilot her through. Keep me coming straight."

"Okay. But if I yell "hit it", give 'er gas and don't let up."

"Roger that," he said as he got into the truck.

Well, with me in front guiding him, Neal made a perfect passage past the bad spot in the road. Once beyond the spring hole, he stopped the truck and I got back in. Then it was off down the logging road to where our trail connected to our route and from there a stroll down the path to fish the fabled waters of Scott Creek.

Vegetation seems to grow at a much faster rate in the Arrowhead than in other places in the United States. I have read about a plant in the Amazon Basin that grows so fast you can actually watch it expand and hear the tissue tearing as the plant swells. Now, the tag alder isn't that prolific, but it does appear to spread and increase at an alarming rate when not kept trimmed by the animals. At any rate, the drivable portion of road ended abruptly, much before our map indicated.

You could make out faint ruts leading off into the tangle, the reminders that vehicles once did ply this road, but unless we cleared a path for our vehicle, we were done driving.

Neal spoke first. "I guess we walk from here."

"Yeah, the trail can't be much more than a half mile from here."

"It looks like the land is dropping off in front of us. That must mean the stream bottom isn't too far from here. Maybe we could strike off cross country?"

"Uh, I don't think that would be a good idea," I answered. "Let's scout it out first, then decide what we're going to do."

"Sounds like a plan."

The walk in would be faster if we left our gear at the truck. We could find the stream and then decide if we were going to spend time fishing it. Even though I was pretty certain this was the access to Scott Creek that my cousin had alluded to, the place may have changed slightly in the last thirty years. Maybe the beavers had dammed it up, maybe it was all silted in or it could have frozen out over a winter. So the decision was made to walk in sans gear and scout it first. If it looked promising, we would hike back to the truck, get our grip and walk back in to fish. If it didn't appear to be a promising stretch of water, we would double time it back to the truck and travel to a different stream to fish.

It only took fifteen hot minutes of walking to get to our goal. The brush began to thin out along the old road until the track was as wide and open as any two-lane highway. A depression that looked like it had been a man-made ditch ran along each side of the road at this point. Here and there, grass, wild strawberry plants and small spring flowers poked out of the old, gravelly road bed. It looked like the ditch had stopped the advance of the tag alder as it abruptly quit growing on the far side of each ditch.

"Look at this," Neal said as he stepped off the side of the byway. "This has been here a while."

"A while" was an understatement for what he was referring to. I looked in the direction he was pointing and saw what had caught his eye. There, in the crotch of an old jack pine was the remnant of a coffee pot. The spout, lid and part of the handle were visible, but the tree had grown around the rest of the old vessel.

"Listen," Neal said.

I took my attention away from the artifact and strained to listen. Then I heard it, too; running water. We both turned and walked toward the middle of the clearing and discovered the source of the sound. There, piercing the roadbed, was an enormous culvert that allowed a small stream to flow from a meadow-like area and off through the forest. The clearing, the meadow and the old coffee pot were signs that people had been here long before us. The map indicated that the stream was Scott Creek. It had to join the Dumbbell River not very far downstream from here.

I was processing all this information when Neal made another discovery. He had walked a short distance off the road to relieve some bladder pressure when he saw it.

"Hey Rudy, come here. This is the place."

I went over to join Neal and to see what he had unearthed. As I approached, he was looking around at the trees and silently counting. Coming closer, I saw them, too. Protruding from a number of trees were square nails of various sizes.

"Look down," he told me.

At the base of one of the trees was a large section of an old cross-cut saw blade that jutted out of the ground at an angle. Scanning around the forest floor I could see bits and pieces of old crockery and metal. The biggest discovery, though, was finding a cast-iron, three-legged pot half buried next to the stream alongside what appeared to be an old log bridge.

"This has to be Fred's lumber camp."

"Yeah, I know. Now we have to decide if we're going to follow the stream first to the river or go right back and get our gear."

Well, we went back and got our gear, then hiked into the confluence of the two streams. There we found a fair-sized pool that backed up against an enormous boulder. I'm thinking that "boulder" or "rock" would have been the next word out of Lee's mouth, if Jason hadn't given him the 'ol stinky eye.

We caught fish that day, but none were close to the size of Fred's trophies. That didn't matter though. We had located a new stretch of water and had gotten the information out of my cousins. What an accomplishment!

Later that summer I had the chance to gloat over prying fishing information out of my relatives. At a family gathering, we were sitting around swapping stories. I slyly interjected Scott Creek into the discussion and then went on to describe in great detail how I had ascertained the location from the sparse information that Jason and Lee had let slip. I went on at great length about my prowess at deduction and what a clever person I was to be able to trick my cousins into relinquishing their secret. I finished my monologue and leaned back smugly in my chair to savor the moment of triumph.

With a smile on his face, Lee looked at me and said, "You know, I never have fished the Dumbbell River. Never been there, actually, but I do fish a place very close to there, and it is incredible." Jason burst out laughing.

I might still have the bruise from where my jaw hit the floor.

Shirley and the Wolves

Life is a series of surprises, and would not be worth taking or keeping if it were not. ~Ralph Waldo Emerson

"Ever been struck with something in your left eye?" my optometrist asked. "There seems to be a large deposit of pigment in there."

We were sitting in his office as he performed my semi-regular eye exam. I had to think back for a moment. No recollection of any eye trauma immediately came to mind.

"Can't think of any.... no, wait," I answered as the memory came slowly back to me. "Yes, I did suffer a blow to that eye twenty years ago. It was during the summer of the big move for Shirley and me. We had a lot going on as we planned our upcoming relocation to Door County"

"Oh," he said as he continued his examination. "What happened? A piece of furniture perhaps or something drop from a box as you were moving?"

"Well, it actually happened in a tent and it was because of the wolves," I casually answered. "Glad we had the fire."

The doctor slowly lowered the instrument he was using to assess some part of my vision. He had a look of surprise on his face, as if what I had just told him were something atypical.

"So," he said, "before we go any further with your exam, let's hear a bit more about this 'incident'. We have some time since I have no more appointments scheduled after yours, and my curiosity may get in the way of an objective exam of your eyes."

"Well, you know that Shirley and I used to head west every summer to backpack and fish," I answered, then stopped and said, "Let me give you a little background to help set the scene."

"By all means," he replied.

He settled back on his stool and I launched into my story.

Shirley and I met in graduate school the summer of 1975. When we weren't in class we spent most of that summer together fishing, camping and hiking. Those things continued to be passions of ours after we married. In those early days we did not own a home and rented places to live during the school year. When school recessed in June, we would vacate our rentals, store all of our belongings, and head west to hike, fish and backpack the mountains. At summer's end, we would return to Wisconsin, locate a place to live for the school year and furnish it with our stored possessions.

She and I continued this pattern every summer, including the year we were expecting our first child. That spring and summer was full of new experiences for us. We were going to be moving from the Milwaukee area to Door County, Wisconsin. Shirley was seven months pregnant and I had been offered a position with the school district of Sturgeon Bay. We were shopping for our first house and had also planned a camping and hiking trip with friends in Colorado. The summer looked pretty full.

That spring, both of us resigned our jobs in southern Wisconsin and began our move north. The first week was spent with a real estate agent as we looked at houses and met with bank representatives to finance our purchase. At the end of that week, we thought we had a home selected. We placed what we felt was a fair offer on the dwelling, gave our agent contact information for us and then headed west. It was agreed that the three of us would connect via telephone once Shirley and I reached Colorado. We planned to arrive three days prior to the others in our hiking group.

The plan was to use these few days to hike and explore the area after which we would rendezvous with four friends from Wisconsin and Idaho at Grand Lake, Colorado. There, the six of us would take a few day hikes together. After that, Shirley would drive to Denver to visit her brother while the rest of us went on a five-day hike in Rocky Mountain National Park.

The strategy made perfect sense to us, and without any outside issues to confound things, it would run smoothly. We would travel west; see some sights, hike, fish, backpack and camp. Shirley and I would reunite with some old friends, and then travel back to Wisconsin to a new job and our first home. What could be more simple?

As usual, the circumstances that one has no control over and does not plan for or anticipate can cause a disruption in the even flow of things.

The first such item presented itself when we called our realtor from Colorado. We were expecting him to tell us when we could actually move into our house. Instead he said, "I've got some bad news for you. The people who own the place that you put an offer on have decided not to sell. What do you want to do?"

What did we want to do, indeed? According to our schedule we would not be back in Wisconsin until the second week of August. School began the third week of August. We had budgeted a week to move into our new home, and now we had no place to move into. On top of that, we were 1000 miles away in Sedgwick, Colorado, it was Friday noon and before the days of the internet.

"What do you suggest?" I asked him.

"Remember that brick home you looked at in Forestville?" he inquired. "It's still available and they have dropped their price."

I had a vague recollection of the place, but we had looked a so many homes that they really all blurred together. I asked him to hold while I told Shirley the story. She remembered the house he was talking about. She calmly said, "Ask him if he thinks it's worth the price. If he says yes, tell him to put an offer on it for us."

He agreed that the house was a value at the asking price and advised us to move ahead. So we did.

"I'll get to them today, and I think I'll have an answer by late afternoon. Will you still be at this number this afternoon?"

"Nope," I answered. "We're still on our way west. Give me a time and I'll call you."

He told us to call him at three o'clock that afternoon and reminded us that we were in a different time zone.

"That means two o'clock your time," he said. "If things go smoothly, we may be able to close this deal today."

With that we said goodbye and I hung up the phone. Shirley and I got back into our truck and continued on our trip. At two o'clock that afternoon we were near Wiggins, Colorado, and began in earnest looking for a public phone; these were the days prior to cell phones. Finally, we located a phone on the outside of a service station/ grocery store/tavern and placed our call.

The answer we got from our real estate agent was positive. The people had accepted our offer, but they wanted to move as quickly as possible to close the deal.

"So, when will you be back in Wisconsin?" our agent asked.

"Well, we're heading into the mountains for two days right after we finish talking with you. Then, we're meeting some friends in Grand Lake and will be in the back country for another five days. With those two trips and driving time, we should be back there in two weeks," I answered.

"I need to have you look over some papers and sign them. Since its Friday, I'd like to get things really rolling before the weekend. Is there a place near you where I can fax those papers?" he asked.

I checked our road map. We would be driving through Greeley, Colorado, on our way to Grand Lake. "How about faxing the papers to a bank in Greeley?" I offered. "We'll be driving right through there and should arrive in about an hour or so. The banks will still be open."

"Hold on, let me check something. I'll be right back."

I heard a soft thud as he put the phone down and then heard the sound of paper being shuffled. He was back on the line in a few minutes.

"Here's the deal. I'm faxing the papers to a Wells Fargo Bank. There are a couple of different ones in Greely, but this one is on 11th Street. Go in, ask for the bank manager and tell him you're the party for the fax. Sign the papers and he'll fax them back to me."

"Got it," I answered. "We'll be there in about an hour."

I hung up the phone and got back into the truck. As we drove off toward Greeley, I filled Shirley in on the plan. The drive went quickly, and soon we were at the bank signing our papers. I jotted a note to our agent on the fax informing him that I would call him Monday, after Shirley and I came out of the mountains. The manager took the papers to fax them, and we exited the building with high spirits as we resumed our drive toward Grand Lake and two days of backpacking.

"So, you got the house?" my doctor asked as he leaned forward to adjust the space-age machinery he was using to assess my eyes.

"Yeah," I said. "And that was one less thing we had to deal with. We continued on our way west with the papers on their way back to Wisconsin."

As my physician made adjustments to the machine my head was clamped into, I continued my story.

We arrived in Grand Lake in late afternoon and eagerly sought information about the area we were considering for our hike. It seemed common sense that Shirley and I check with the rangers about local conditions. After locating their office, we met with a ranger and posed our questions. Were the trails in good shape? Was there a concern for bears? Were there many people using the trailhead we had chosen? What shape were the campsites in and was there potable water near them? What was the fishing report for the area?

The two of us got the answers we wanted to all of our questions. We were told that the trails were in great shape and that even though Shirley was seven months pregnant, she should have no trouble. Very few people were using the route we had chosen, the campsites were in great condition and they had a supply of water nearby. As for bears, there were none reported in the area, and we didn't have to search out a bear tree for hanging our food.

It was too late in the day to begin our hike, so we decided to camp near the trailhead that night. Our sojourn into the Rockies would commence after breakfast on the following morning. We could sleep in the back of the pickup and wouldn't have to set up a tent, which would help expedite breaking camp in the morning.

The evening passed quickly as we ate and prepared. We moved our gear out of the back of the pick-up to store overnight in the cab. That made room in the small topper shell for our bedrolls.

We arose with the early sun and after a quick breakfast we were on our way. The day was bright and the sky clear as we ascended the trail into the park. Our destination was Cascade Falls, a moderate three and a half mile hike along the East Inlet Trail. We thought we would take our time getting to the falls, camp overnight in the area, possibly get some evening fishing in and then hike back out the following day. Since we wouldn't need much extra clothing or a lot of food, our packs were fairly light.

We took our time and enjoyed many stops to take in the scenery and to enjoy a leisurely lunch alongside East Inlet Creek. Shirley did get some gap-mouthed stares from the folks we met on the way in. Seeing someone seven months pregnant with a sizeable back pack on must have seemed odd to them.

We arrived at Cascade Falls in the early afternoon. After dropping our packs, we searched for a level place and pitched our tent. Shirley arranged the interior of our little shelter while I scouted around for firewood. I didn't have to look very hard since the ground was littered with dry branches and pine cones.

By the time the sun slid behind the mountain peaks and the shadows crept across the ground, we had a snug little campsite setup and a friendly fire going. Shirley and I sat by our fire drinking hot cider as we let the flames slowly die out to glowing embers.

With the light from the fire gone, the brilliance and closeness of the stars became more obvious. The sky seemed ablaze with the blue and white icy fire that they provided. We watched the sky and saw occasional shooting stars until the change in temperature became noticeable through our fleece jackets.

"It's getting chilly and late," I said. "Let's turn in."

"What about the fire?" Shirley asked as she gestured toward the bed of glowing coals.

"It won't go anywhere. We'll have a nice bed of coals to start the fire in the morning. We can bank up the sides and leave it til then."

We moved our packs under the tent's rain fly just in case there was any bad weather during the night. Then, after visiting the local restroom (behind the nearest pine tree), we grabbed our water bottles and crawled into the tent.

We had pitched our tent away from the trail and under a stand of pines. Our thoughts were that, should it rain during the night, the trees would give us and our gear a bit more protection from the water. The trees also blocked any view of the sky and what ambient light the stars provided, so we were immersed in almost total darkness when we entered our tent.

The coolness within our bags quickly changed as our bodies heated up the inside and we were soon wrapped in a very snug and warm cocoon. Almost immediately, we were both sound asleep.

"Well, so far it sounds like a regular hike into the mountains," my doctor said as he jotted down a few notes.

"Yeah, well that's what we thought too," I replied. "But the evening's entertainment had not yet begun."

It is difficult, if not impossible, to judge the passing of time while you are sleeping. I have awakened after lying down and thought the night to be half over only to find out after checking my watch that I had been asleep for just an hour or less. Other times I awake and feel as though I had just lain down and discover it is morning.

This night I was aroused from a deep sleep by Shirley whispering, "Rick! Rick! Wake up."

There was urgency in her voice, but she was speaking in low tones as if she didn't want anyone else to hear what she was saying.

"What's up?" I mumbled in my half-awake voice.

"I heard dogs," was her reply.

My cognitive ability began to sharpen as the shroud of sleep slowly left my body. I listened for any sounds, but there were none. It was so still I could only hear the blood pounding in my temples as I lay there in the tent.

"You're dreaming," I replied. "We're in the mountains, miles from the truck. There aren't any dogs up here. Go back to sleep."

The words had no sooner exited my mouth when snarling and growling erupted right outside the tent. The sounds of scuffling and material being torn were interspersed with what sounded like a dog fight.

I processed this information in a millisecond. I knew we were in an emergency situation, I assumed we had wolves or at the very least, coyotes, tearing into our packs. I needed to get rid of them and protect my pregnant wife. In one fluid movement, I sat up in my sleeping bag, hit the side of the tent with my fist and screamed, "Get the hell out of here!"

The sounds outside the tent ceased.

"What do you think happened?" Shirley asked me.

"Something was going after our packs. They must have smelled the peanut butter in the tubes or something else. I think the noise scared them away. Grab a flashlight for me and I'll go outside and check the damages."

I lay back down in my bag and reached along my sides to get my socks. Shirley got out of her bag and moved toward the front of the tent to get her flashlight. Usually, we stored our flashlights inside of the tent door next to our boots. That way they were there if we needed to exit our shelter at night for a restroom break. Tonight, however, we had put our flashlights inside of our boots and had put our boots just outside the tent door under the rain flap.

The next few moments happened very fast. I had retrieved my socks and was in the process of sitting up to put them on. Shirley had reached the tent door and had started to zip it open. Her movement of the tent door must have startled the creature that was sitting outside the door under our rain flap because it snarled and barked at the moving tent. This prompted an instantaneous reaction in Shirley. She simultaneously screamed, jumped backwards and snatched her arm away from the door. The rest was physics. I think the principle is that for every action there is an equal and opposite reaction.

Shirley and her elbow were traveling toward the rear of the tent at a certain speed while I was sitting up at another rate. Her elbow collided with my eye socket.

What I remember next was a blinding white flash of light, a sickening crunching sound and my head being hurled back to the floor of the tent. Shirley tells me that I loudly verbalized my displeasure and discomfort at being hit in the eye, but I don't remember doing so. However, when my moaning stopped, I realized that there were no other sounds coming from outside of our tent.

Shirley began to apologize profusely for the mishap.

"Let's get outside and take a look," I said. "It was an accident and we're both okay."

With that, I cautiously opened the tent door, grabbed a flashlight and switched it on. As an afterthought, I reached back and grabbed my pocket knife. Since I was in my underwear and socks, I didn't have a pocket to put it in, so I tucked it inside of one of my socks. I don't know how really useful that knife would have been, but it gave me a sense of security that I was armed.

We both crawled out of the tent and swept the area with our flashlight beams. Our packs had been dragged a short distance from the tent, and except for a few minor tears in one, they were in good shape.

Our fire had burned down to a bed of glowing embers. I handed Shirley my flashlight and grabbed some duff from the ground to use to build up the fire. It didn't take long to get it blazing again. The light from the flames illuminated the area around our clearing and back to the tent. It cast shadows from the trees and us, and also picked up the luminosity in the eyes of our tormentors. The wolves, as we now realized they were, had retreated back into the forest and were passively sitting just outside the ring of light that the fire threw.

I grabbed a wrist-sized stick from the ground and hurled it at one of the sets of glowing eyes. The effect was not what I wanted. The animal jumped up at the approach of the missile and moved a few feet, then sat back down again.

According to everything I knew and had read, wolves were supposed to shun humans and run when confronted like that. Evidently these wolves hadn't read the same books I had. They were content to sit there and wait. Obviously they really were interested in our packs, but true to my readings, not so much in the fire.

"What are we going to do?" Shirley asked.

"Well, I guess we stay up and keep the fire going. I'm sure they'll take off come daylight."

"You were sure they would run away when you threw that stick, too."

"Yeah, well, I'm sure they'll take off. We just keep the fire going and we collect everything to burn that is in our ring of light. We can take turns sleeping and watching the fire."

"Oh, I couldn't sleep now," she said.

"Give it a shot. I'll be out here. I'll wake you in a couple of hours. Try to get some rest."

Reluctantly, Shirley crawled back into the tent. In a matter of minutes, the sounds of deep breathing emanated from our little shelter. So much for her not getting to sleep.

I checked my watch for the time. 2:30 in the morning. The sun would be peeking over the mountains by 5:30 and with predawn light a little before that there was no need to wake Shirley for fire duty.

I spent that early morning standing in my underwear and socks tending our fire. The darkness slowly passed into daylight. At some time during the night, the wolves had faded back into the wilderness and when it became light, the only reminder that they had been at our campsite were the tears in our packs and some teeth marks in our tubes of peanut butter.

I looked around our tent and fire pit and realized I had burned every piece of available fuel in the immediate area. There were not any pieces of wood larger than a matchstick lying around on the ground.

"So, I'm assuming you broke camp and got out of there," said my optometrist.

"Well, the wolves were gone, it was a beautiful day, and we were in no hurry," I answered. "So we had a mixed breakfast of what food we had left, then broke camp and began our walk out."

"Well, did you see a doctor in town?" he asked me.

"For what?"

"Your eye. Didn't it bother you?"

"Oh, it was a little sensitive to light, but I put a patch over it and that helped a lot. It also made for some good stories when we met up with other people."

My optometrist just silently stared at me for a moment. Slowly he shook his head from side to side, then picked up his medical pad and wrote a prescription for new lenses.

"Wolves, a pregnant wife, blinded in one eye and in the mountains. Well, that's an interesting story, Rudy, thanks for sharing it with me."

"No problem. But, what about my eye? Should I be concerned about that pile of pigment in my left eye?"

"No, just watch out for elbows."

The Honey Hole

"Memory is the treasure house of the mind wherein the monuments thereof are kept and preserved"
~Thomas Fuller

The late night sky had been so clear that the stars were able to illuminate our trail into the stream. As we approached the meadow that our destination cut a course through, dawn was beginning to lighten the horizon. I had never been on this stretch of water before, but Arvo had declared it to be "The honey hole of all honey holes". So, putting my trust in my best friend's hands, I had agreed to get up before dawn and drive two hours north with him in order to be at this spot before sunrise.

"It's only about half a mile in," Arv had told me. "The trail is easy to follow; the moose have been using it. As far as I can see, no one has fished this place in years."

"So, how did you find it?" I had asked.

He launched into a story about his grandfather and his father. His grandfather had been a land cruiser. His job was to walk the land and mark various areas for cutting or for surveying. Arvo's father had accompanied his grandfather on many of those traverses It was during one of those cross country walks that the two of them had crossed Egge Creek. It was "just a little trickle" according to Arv's dad, but there were lots of pools and deep spots that could hold some nice fish.

"Your dad ever fish it?" I asked.

"Just once. He limited in twenty minutes. Then, he went back in the evening and limited again. After that trip he never got back there though, and that was over thirty years ago."

This was beginning to sound like a real "dream" place. But, if no one had been in there for over thirty years, what would the trail going in, if any, be like? Yet, Arv assured me it was a piece of cake to get in there. I should have reasoned out that if it was so easy, everybody and their brother would have been fishing that place. But, visions of monster trout tend to cloud over the reasoning part of my brain and I never questioned him.

Arv picked me up at my house at 3:00 in the morning. If everything went as planned, that departure time would put us at the trailhead at roughly 5:00, which would give us plenty of time to walk to the creek and be there before sun up. Luck was with us on our drive that morning. We did not encounter any errant moose or early morning logging equipment that might have delayed us.

Arv slowed the truck down as we approached the gravel pit that was near the place where the old landing of Maple had once been. He leaned forward toward the dashboard as he squinted out of the windshield and tried to pick out any familiar landmarks that the headlights illuminated.

"There it is," he said as he braked. "See that old culvert? We walk in from here."

"Is THAT the stream?" I asked, referring to the tiny trickle of water that coursed out of the forest and into the culvert.

"Naw. That's a run-off from the marsh. It gets pretty mushy right here off the road. We need to skirt that low area and follow the high ground in until we get to the meadows. The main stream flows through that meadows and there's a pretty fair game trail along the edge of that ridge that we can follow. Then we'll cut straight for the stream."

Arv killed the ignition and the two of us climbed out of the truck. We dropped the tailgate and sat on it while we changed from our shoes to hip boots. The rubber was cool from the night air and gave us each a slight chill as our warm feet slid into them. Our body heat would warm the boots before we got to the water. We pulled them on and rolled the boot tops down to knee height for our walk through the forest. That being done we donned our vests and grabbed our rods and flashlights. After a final equipment check before locking the truck, we were off along the path into the forest.

The game trail Arv mentioned was very well traveled by the local ungulates. The path was worn downs into the forest floor several inches deep in many places as the animals had been following the edge of the marsh for years. Our flashlight beams slashed through the darkness under the trees and cast ghostly shadows into the depths of the forest. Wherever the black spruce and tamarack trees thinned out a bit, the starlight illuminated our way as well.

Although the sounds of our footfalls were muffled by the needles and soft moss covering the ground, we startled a large animal from its rest and heard the beast crashing off through the dark underbrush. Aside from our audible gasp at that moment, we didn't talk on the way in.

Soon we began encountering patches of ground fog indicating our closeness to the meadow clearing. The rising mist thickened closer to the tree line. Looking ahead we could see the vapor rising, ghostlike, in our flashlight beams. It was especially thick along the course of the stream, lying over the top of the stream like a heavy blanket completely obscuring our view of the water.

I have seen early morning ground fog many times in my life and that sight always brings to mind a story my father told me when I was a very young boy. It was early evening near the old Big Lake, Minnesota, cemetery. He and I had been driving along the Big Lake Road on our way home from a spring fishing trip. Daylight had faded and the moon had begun to rise. On either side of the road the low, wet land was sparsely covered with the skeletons of drowned out black ash trees. Their bare branches reached for the sky and cast eerie shadows in the moonlight. The evening mist had begun to form and wisps of fog seemed to glow with a white light as they rose from the swampy landscape.

My father saw me looking out of the car window at the rising evening mist and began to talk about it. He didn't share any scientific information about warm and cold air masses and moisture. If he had, I don't know that I would have listened or even remembered our conversation.

"Wonder if we'll see a Will-o-the-wisp tonight." He said.

"A what?"

"Ghost light," my father casually answered.

"GHOST LIGHT?!?" I croaked.

"Yeah. Usually around here you can see them because of the old cemetery."

"What???"

My dad launched into the story of the lights. You could usually see them at this time of night in the area we were driving through, he told me. According to the local legend, a Native American medicine woman was tricked and killed by a jealous suitor. She was buried somewhere nearby close to a big old tree. At twilight her spirit rises from her grave and searches for the person who deceived her. She tries to coax unwary travelers to follow her glowing apparition into the swamp. Those that are duped into following her are never seen again.

"Really?" I asked.

"Well, I'll never follow the wisp into the woods," he said

That legend has stayed with me through all my years of crisscrossing the forests. This dark morning as Arv and I waded through the rising mist in the meadow, I could not help but think of that medicine woman. I hadn't reflected on her very long when Arv's low whisper brought me back.

"We need get into the creek just below that bunch of tag alder," he hissed.

I squinted through the dim light of early morning and could make out a dark mass near the edge of the fog blanket.

"When we get to the creek, ease in, don't splash. The water is shallow there. We'll walk about fifty feet upstream to the backside of a gravel bar. Take your time; we don't want to spook the fish."

Arv and I slowly made our way through that eerie landscape to the bank of the stream. The flowage didn't look like a "little trickle" as Arv's father had said. On the contrary, it was a nice sized stream, roughly ten feet wide at this particular place.

Our entrance into the water was smooth and silent. I followed Arv as he cautiously waded upstream toward where he had said there was a gravel bar. Fifty feet isn't a great distance, but time did seem to slow down as we worked our way against the current. The water sang softly as it danced over the pebbles which also helped cover any noise made by our progress.

"Here we are," Arv said motioning toward something in front of him.

I moved up next to him and could see that there was a small mound in front of us.

"There's waist high grass growing in the middle of this thing," he said. "We need to walk up over the bar and keep low. When we get to the other side, we'll stop while we're still in cover and cast from there. The pool on the backside of the bar is deep at the far end but comes up gradually to where we'll be. The trout lie in the drop-off at the other end, just where the fast water comes into the pool. We can tie up here so we're ready," he added.

Arv began rummaging in his vest pockets for something suitable.

"What are you going to use?" I asked him.

"Grasshopper," he replied. "The meadow is full of them and once the sun comes up they'll be jumping all over. What about you?"

"I was thinking something wet, like a stone fly nymph," I said.

"Not here," he replied casually. "Got a muddler?"

"Yeah, but the ones I have are size eight and six."

"Use a six," he said as he continued to rig his gear.

He must have seen my look of disbelief in the dim light, or he just sensed that I had some doubt about his recommendation.

"Trust me," he said and bit off the extra tippet line that dangled below the knot he had tied.

I rummaged in my vest pockets and located the fly box that houses my larger flies. Opening it, I quickly selected a grey-brown monstrosity and began to tie it on.

"We need to snap it up," Arv said. "Sun's coming up and we want to be casting when it hits the tree tops."

I looked up and saw that he was right. The horizon directly in front of us was beginning to lighten, changing from the blackness of night to the steel-blue that precedes sunrise. I hastily finished my knot and let Arv know I was ready. Without a word he slowly began his ascent from the water to the dry rocks and pebbles of the bar. I followed.

The gravel deposit was shaped like an elongated egg. The upstream end was rounded and the small island tapered to a point on the downstream side. Crouching low to keep shielded by the grass, we scuttled across the top of the gravel bar then stopped and kneeled at the grass's edge on the far side.

"We'll throw from here," Arv told me. "It's a little tricky casting from your knees, but you don't need to toss it too far and that helps. Wait a couple of minutes until the sun gets a little higher. The fog is already starting to lift some but we want it up a little more."

As the sun slowly rose and shed more light through the trees and onto the meadow, the pool in front of us became more visible. The sun was rising directly in front of us, and reflecting off of the water's surface. It gave the stream a metallic silver sheen which obscured any chance we had to see below the surface.

"Boy, it's going to be tough to see where to cast. Can't see the fish."

"They can't see us either," was Arv's reply. "My dad said they're usually at the throat of the pool, so we cast toward there. Give the sun about five more minutes, and we start casting. Take a peek over the grass top," he finished. "And be careful, go slow."

Carefully I raised my head and peered over the top of the grass. The smooth, steely-blue water lay before me. As I started to lower my head back into the cover, I noticed some minor disturbance to the surface of the stream.

"Arv! There's fish swirling at the end of the pool."

"They break the surface?" he asked.

"Just a little, no splash."

"They're tailing," he said. "Chasing minnows or crawfish probably. Perfect for us. Let me tie on a different pattern, then we'll hit the water together. Once either of us splashes the pool, the fishing here will be done for a while."

He quickly changed fly patterns and tied on something he called a "haystack". It was supposed to resemble a variety of aquatic life. To me it looked like a bunch of deer hair wrapped around a hook, but I wasn't the one to be enticed by it.

Once Arv had his pole rigged we started our casts. He and I did a fairly good job of coordinating our false casts and then shooting our flies out over the pool. The two imitation bugs landed on opposite sides of the entrance to the pool within a second of each other. We began to strip the line, bringing our lures back across the depths of the pool and toward where we knelt, concealed by the grass.

A fish struck Arv's hairy concoction first. I couldn't believe a fish hit that ugly fly. But my attention was snapped back to my own fishing when I felt a sudden surge on my line. We had doubled, both having a fish on at the same time. Our quarries raced to opposite sides of the pool, then dashed for the gravel bar as they tried to head downstream.

"Tip up! Tip up!" Arv yelled as a reminder to me. He stood up and retreated along the gravel bar trying to hold his rod straight up as it arced and pointed down the stream.

I also came to a standing position and followed my fish around the other side of the gravel bar. There was no reason to remain concealed now that we had stirred up and spooked the upper pool with our fish. Any others that had been there would be gone by now.

My fish gave a couple of good runs, then rolled to its side and I reeled it in. Arv, however, was still wading downstream, chasing his fish. I lost sight of him as he rounded the bend in the stream just below the gravel bar.

We had not talked about what kind of trout we would be fishing. My assumption was brook trout, since they were the species that seemed to be predominant in these waters. But as I reeled my catch toward my net I realized this was not a brookie. This fish was huge by brook trout standards and the colors weren't right. The fish was caramel-brown in color with huge red, orange and black spots. This was a brown trout and a beautiful one at that. It never occurred to me that we would catch brown trout in this creek.

As I stood there gazing at my fish as it lay on the edge of the gravel bar, I heard Arv sloshing his way up the stream toward me.

"Dya get 'em?" I yelled.

"Yeah, wait 'til you see this," He answered.

Arv came walking around the bend in the creek. He smiled from ear to ear.

"Look at this guy," he said as he lifted his fish toward me beaming.

My brown trout was an impressive fish, close to 16 inches in length. However, Arv's was a monster. His measured 20 inches long, but had a girth and depth that were phenomenal. We weighed the fish when we got back to Two Harbors later that day and it tipped the scales at just less than five pounds.

The two of us fished the remainder of the morning on that creek and left when the sun got high. Arv and I caught a number of smaller trout that day but we released them all. It didn't matter. There was no way we could top what had happened earlier on that gravel bar.

I never got a chance to go back to those waters. That trip happened over thirty years ago in 1975, and it's still clear in my mind. I like it that way. The intoxication of walking through the morning mist that day could never be duplicated, and the fish get a little bigger and more colorful with each telling.

The Bottle

"The footprints you leave behind will influence others. There is no person who at some time, somewhere, somehow, does not lead another." ~ *Anonymous*

It must have lain on the forest floor since before I was born. Clear, bluish glass, with the remnants of a cork lodged in the neck, the little bottle glittered as it caught a stray ray of sunshine. It was all alone, on its side, on a bed of damp, green moss as if someone had placed it there on display. Had I not stopped to check my compass, most likely I would have walked by without ever seeing the little artifact.

"Hey, Neal, come check this out," I yelled ahead to my companion.

Neal stopped, turned back toward me and asked, "What's up?"

"There's an old bottle lying here. Looks like a liniment or ointment bottle of some kind."

He turned and came back through the brush to where I was standing to look at my find. As I waited I became aware of the heady scent around me. The warm afternoon air had loosened the resin in the cedar needles and the fragrance of the trees wafted through the air.

We were at the end of a great day of fishing on one of our favorite stretches of water and had started back to our truck following a well used moose trail that paralleled the stream. In all the years we had been fishing this particular area, we had never come across any sign that some other person had visited there. But here, today, was the evidence that we were not the only ones ever on this particular creek.

We knew the area had been logged over in the early part of the century, so humans had been through here before us. However, nature had done her part in reclaiming the land and most traces of that habitation had been swallowed back up by the forest.

Our route into the creek followed the remains of an old winter road that had been cut years ago by lumbermen. Now the only indication that it had existed was that the brush along this route was shorter than the surrounding vegetation. Animals had adopted the old road and used it as a trail of their own, keeping a narrow rudimentary path open through the tag alder.

But before getting to the remnants of the winter road, we had driven three miles along an ancient railbed which the folks at the forestry department had told us was impassible. It was from the end point of the railbed that we walked a mile along the game trail to where it crossed the flowage.

I picked up the bottle and lifted it to the sunlight. Any semblance of a label had long ago weathered away. But held that way I could read the raised letters on the flat face of the bottle. Except for the embossed lettering, there was no identification on the vessel.

"It says, Foley & Company, Chicago, on the front," I said to Neal. "Nothing else. Looks like there's a waxy residue still inside though."

I handed the relic to Neal, who turned it slowly in his hands as he inspected our find.

I have said many times that the trips to the Arrowhead to fish for brook trout are really about more than just the fish alone. While tramping through what we think is a trackless wilderness to gain access to a secluded portion of a river, we sometimes make a surprise discovery that turns our trek for fish into something more.

"Wow. I wonder how long this thing has been here?"

It was a rhetorical question, but it made us pause. On many trips through the Arrowhead in the past, we had come across artifacts left by others. But those relics usually were usually at the end of an old road or trail. The places we had stumbled upon before were areas where groups of individuals had resided. Companies of lumberjacks, small settlements of people or families homesteading would leave their obvious mark on the land. While the forest reclaimed some of the land they lived on, it was apparent that people had once been there. Finding the outlines of buildings, piles of discarded materials, or equipment left behind because of wear or disrepair had not been uncommon for us.

Finding this bottle was different. It was lying on its side, under a thick stand of cedar trees about twenty feet from the stream bank. There was no evidence the water ever got high enough to wash it so far into the forest. We looked around and scuffed up the surface of the forest floor in any area that appeared as if it could be an old dump of some sort, but found nothing else man-made. Further searching showed us that there was no trail, road or remnant of either in proximity to this site. There were some remains of pine stumps showing the flat surface indicating they had been cut and not the victims of some wind storm or other natural catastrophe. The wood that remained in them was rotten and crumbled easily to the touch.

Tag alder and thorn apple grew close to the edge of the water and slowly gave way to a stand of large cedars inland. Actually, large doesn't do the cedars justice. They were enormous. If Neal and I stood on either side of one we could just stretch our arms far enough to touch finger tips as we reached around them. These giants were easily 60 to 70 years old or more. They must have been saplings, if there at all, when the bottle was dropped on the forest floor.

According to the history books, this region was at the peak of logging operations in 1900, and most people knew that Minnesota was running out of pine. The statistics indicate that at least 20,000 lumberjacks were working in the pineries along with half that number of horses. Alger-Smith Company narrow gauge railroads ran from Duluth to Tow Island Lake and transported the logs from the waterways and landings to their sawmills in Duluth. When the largest white pine lumber company in the world at that time, the Rainy River Lumber Company in Virginia, Minnesota, closed its doors in 1929, logging pretty much came to a close here.

The companies retrieved the rails from the old railbeds and used them as they moved north and west in pursuit of white pine. They left the old spikes and rail ties behind. Many were covered when the right of ways were graded over for the roads that now provide access to Cramer and Finland. But others were abandoned and along with the cleared land, were reclaimed by the forest. The philosophy of the plow following the ax did not work well here since the soil was much too poor for sustainable farming. Second growth forest spread through the clearings, and sturdy tag alder sprouted up through the old road beds.

Those overgrown byways now provided access to the streams in the area. I had walked many of them with Doivo when I was young as he showed me the secret places to fish for brook trout. That was how I first became aware of the stream we had fished today.

When you stand among the old cedars and ponder the size of the northern forest, you can feel very insignificant. It's as though the forest has consumed you, and for a moment you can grasp the power of nature. It reminds you that the earth doesn't belong to mankind, but that mankind belongs to the earth. Regardless of any human's attempts to tame her in the end nature always wins.

But, what was the story behind the old bottle? How did it come to rest in this remote place? Who dropped or threw it here so long ago? Although this makes for some entertaining discussion, there seldom is any specific proof that other people have been there. But this time there was.

We can only speculate at who the person was who left the bottle, and that is part of what makes trips to the Arrowhead so intoxicating. Our best guess is a lumberjack or timber cruiser who passed through during their day's labor. Humans wandered these forests when the waterways and game trails were the only routes through them. Yet there are times when, for just a moment, Neal and I wonder if we are the first people to cross a certain pathway. At those moments it feels as if the wilderness has swallowed us; just as it has swallowed the stories of those who came before us.

I thought about the difference in how we viewed this land. Neal and I fish the waters and marveled at the beauty and the strength of the native brookies. We pause occasionally to drink in the magnificence and solitude of the wilderness. Our counterpart, the bottle owner, probably paused to touch up the edge on his ax or to clean the pitch from the teeth of his saw blade, then, not to waste the daylight, get back to his labor. He was here to do a job the white pines meant income to him and his family if he had one.

If it had been a lumberjack, he would have been here during the winter months when the ground was frozen hard. The going through the brush would be a bit easier but the days could be bitterly cold. A cruiser, on the other hand, would come through during the spring or summer and have to deal with other issues. The heat and the thick growth would be a challenge, but the insects would be terrible. Could this bottle be some potion to help ward off the attack of the blood-thirsty mosquitoes and black flies? It might have provided a more soothing ointment than the balsam sap and bacon grease combination that the early loggers slathered on to slow down the bug onslaught.

"Boy, if that bottle could talk," I mused.

Neal nodded in agreement.

It was just a small glass bottle, and it probably had a fascinating story, but we were never to know what that was. It began its journey in Chicago, but now it lay on a bed of moss and was a tiny mystery of the Arrowhead. Neal handed it to me and I placed it back on the moss pillow where it rested for those many years. There are some treasures that you can take from the forest, but there are others that should be left where they lie. A quick look around, and we walked away.

To us, that small container will remain another indication of man's attempt to shape and domesticate this wild area. We feel fortunate that places such as this still exist and have not been tamed. These locations have a certain sanctity and purity to them. The price we pay to be able to use these places is simple. When we leave those sites, the only reminders that people have been there are the old cut marks, the tracks we may have made and an occasional small bottle.

The Day the Beagle Ate My Hat

It's always the badly dressed people who are the most interesting. ~Jean Paul Gaultier

"I've got something that you might like," Wayne said to me as we sat around the kitchen table one evening at Crooked Lake Resort. "I bought it when I owned that resort in Canada. I don't have much use for it, so if you could use it, it's yours."

Having said that he went over to his duffel bag, reached in, and pulled out a small box. On the side was printed, Garmin GPSMAP76S.

Was he serious? I couldn't quite believe that he wanted to give me a new GPS, but as it turned out, that is exactly what he wanted to do. This was a piece of technology that was light years ahead of the equipment I was used to.

Proper equipment is very important to a successful and hassle-free fishing trip. Traditionally, during our evening downtime we brainstorm what piece of equipment we think would help take the toil out of our expeditions.

Over the years, Neal, Ryan and I have added something unique and ground-breaking each season. However, some of the revolutionary new equipment did not stand up to the claims that the manufacturers made, nor the rigorous standards we demanded from it.

The lightweight, seamless, water-tight waders that I purchased from a gas station survived only one trip into the brush. No amount of duct tape could stem the flow that poured through the multiple punctures in them after that excursion. The "Wonder-Boner" turned out to be less than we expected. The only "wonder" from that gadget was how it not only didn't remove the bones from our catch but seemed to multiply the amount in the animal's original skeletal structure.

Due to our creative nature, lack of finances and the necessity to get things done in a hurry, there were times we tried to improvise pieces of equipment. Having adequate raingear is an example that comes to mind.

On a beautiful early summer day in June, 1972, Neal and I made an afternoon trip up the Northshore to fish. We had already put in a long morning at St. Joseph's Children's Home, a statewide residential center for Wisconsin court adjudicated youth. There were two buildings to house the children and the classrooms on the 22 acre site. Built in the later part of the 1800's, it was on the town border in a wooded, secluded area. The facility is deserted today and the Superior has grown around what was then the very edge of town. I was the wood shop instructor there and Neal was a resident counselor. We met while chaperoning a field trip with the clients from the home and discovered that both of us were passionate trout fishermen.

That day we knew we would be on the water until just about dark and would not have time for supper. Because the amount of time we fished was critical we wanted to cut out any unnecessary tasks. Packing something to take along to eat would cut into our travel or fishing time. Instead we decided we would stop in Finland at the Fighting Bullhead Tavern and pick up some snacks. There was a little grocery department in those days, complete with a small meat cooler. We could get our provisions there on our way to fish the Hockamin.

Instead of bringing along bulky raincoats, which would take up valuable space in our creels, we opted for a quick alternative. Each of us carried a large, rolled-up lawn bag to use as a substitute. In the event of rain, we would cut holes in the bag for our heads and arms and pull the makeshift shelter over us. We could continue fishing and be dry.

We discovered during our first torrential downpour that the bags formed a very functional funnel that channeled water down our backs and into the tops of our hip boots. No amount of readjusting or customizing could eliminate this design flaw. We eventually gave in to the design shortcomings, stowed the bag/raincoats in our vest pockets and continued to fish in the rain.

The failures of some apparatus we tested over the years did not discourage us from continuing to look for innovative advances into technology for sampling the aquatic vertebrates that inhabited the waters of the Arrowhead. But, of all the clothing, equipment, and paraphernalia I have acquired over the years, the one piece of gear I consider essential is some type of hat.

Hats have been around for a long time and have served many purposes; symbols of status, fashion statements and as a functional piece of protective headgear. The hats that I have possessed fit into all three of those categories. They have been of various designs and have all functioned well.

I did not wear a hat when I fished as a youngster, but over the years came to the realization that covering my head could sometimes be an advantage. Days of fishing in a downpour, having the top of my head feel like it is being baked by the sun, or squinting in the bright sunlight as I fished all helped bring me to that awareness. I also noticed all the older fishermen I knew wore a hat of some kind when they ventured out on the streams and lakes.

Combining all those nuggets of information, I deduced that a hat was probably beneficial to a fisherman. Thus began my quest for THE hat. In fashion terms, a hat is a very noticeable accessory because the onlooker's attention is first drawn to the face. Mine had to be functional yet not look tasteless and still communicate that I was a seasoned fisherman.

I went to the Gambles Hardware store in my home town and began my shopping. After trying on several different head-coverings, I settled on one I thought fit my requirements. It was dead-grass brown in color and looked like the hat Robin Hood or one of his merry men would wear- sans feather.

I paid for the hat and wore it home. Once there I looked through all of my father's flies to find one I could use to decorate my new apparel. I chose an old Royal Coachman I knew he would never miss and impaled the fly through the center of my hat's brim. My chapeau was now complete. That head-piece lasted me through college, but then had to be retired. I hated to put it away for the last time, but the Royal Coachman had deteriorated to just a rusty hook in what remained of the brim. From years of wear in all sorts of weather, the hat's original color was anyone's guess.

The clothes that outdoorsmen wear take on a personality of their own. Not donning a certain shirt or hat gives a different, sometimes uncomfortable feeling on an outing. Discarding a piece of clothing takes months and sometimes years of soul-searching and thought before it can be finally thrown away even if it has already been replaced. Such was the case with my first hat. I had purchased a new, suitable cap to wear, but had not abandoned my first one.

I draped my old friend on a hook near the back door to my house. My wife didn't appreciate the old hat and made no bones about it, often referring to "that useless scrap on the back hall hook". But I would no sooner discard a family member than to toss that cap into the trash. It hung there as if at rest, always bidding me good luck when I left to hunt or fish and greeting me on my return home. Until one day it disappeared.

I can't say for certain exactly when it went missing since I didn't check on it daily. But one Saturday as I prepared to leave for a fishing trip, I noticed my old companion was gone, the hook was bare.

"Where's my hat?" I asked from the back door.

"You're wearing it," came the answer.

"No, I mean the one that was on the hook."

"That old tan rag? Don't know. Maybe it crawled off somewhere to die," came a somewhat sarcastic reply from my spouse.

I searched the floor, the hall closets, I even looked in the trash just in case my suspicion was true, but I could find no trace of my hat.

"You never wear it. Why do you want it today?"

I didn't answer the question. I knew if you had to ask, you would never understand the answer anyway. I never saw that hat again.

Over the years I have had similar things happen to favorite fishing pants or shirts. They would get a bit torn, stained, or threadbare over the years of use even though that didn't affect the functionality of the piece of clothing. At least that was my perspective. I would wear the same outfits year after year, and at season's end I would carefully put them away to await the spring. However, come spring, when I would pack for my first trip, some of the items would have vanished. Try as I may I could never get any help in locating the missing items.

"Hey, have you seen those khaki pants? The ones with the blood stain on the thigh?"

The response was always the same, "They must be right where you put them."

I finally stopped asking the question and just accepted that those clothes must now be in that "great clothing closet in the sky", the place where all good broken in garments go.

I progressed through various head coverings over the years, but never found one that felt as perfect as that first model I had owned. Rummage sales, salvage shops or clothing stores just couldn't produce a suitable topknot. The feel or the cut was just not right. Through the years I continued the quest for the hat that was "just right". I knew that somewhere it existed, and if I looked long enough I would find it. And that is just what happened.

My family had grown to a wife, two daughters and a beagle inherited from my mother. The dog, Susie, was a friendly, playful animal but had an inquisitive streak that was sometimes annoying, particularly when it came to articles of clothing. She liked to gather shirts, socks and assorted other clothing items and build a nest for herself to curl up on to sleep. Susie was especially fond of my fishing apparel.

I have discovered that the end-of-season sales are a great place to find equipment at reasonable prices. Therefore, I make every attempt to peruse the stores after fishing season in an attempt to replenish my gear for the following year. Shirley is much more tolerant of my fashion sense than any other person I have known and she is always there to help me decide which outdoor clothes will be the best "fit".

At a bargain basement sale in late October I found the perfect replacement hat. It was sitting atop a pile of equipment on a table near the back of the shop. The hat was brown felt with a wide brim and a brown satin hatband. It looked just like the hat Mark Trail, the outdoorsman from the comic strip of my youth, would wear.

I slowly walked toward the table to more closely examine my find. It was in perfect shape, it fit me comfortably and best yet, it was marked 80% off the original price. I modeled the hat for Shirley, who approved. However, before I could purchase it, she reminded me that she was looking for gift ideas for Christmas. Would I mind if she purchased the hat for me and then put it away until the holidays? I thought this over for a millisecond and agreed that it sounded like a great idea.

I did get the hat that Christmas and wore it for the better part of the evening, much to the chagrin of my family. I explained I was attempting to bond with my new chapeau and trying to get it to form to my head. My explanation resulted in smirks and eye-rolling from my wife and daughters. But no matter, I had a new hat, one that fit just right and also helped me look dashing and dapper, I thought. Wait until my fishing partners saw it in the spring.

Our holiday festivities slowly wound down that evening until yawns and drooping heads indicated we were all ready to turn in for the night.

"You gonna sleep in that thing, dad?" one of my daughters asked.

"That would be crazy. It can stay here under the tree with the other gifts."

"Yeah, but wearing it all evening certainly isn't crazy," came a reply from one of my family members.

I lovingly placed my gift under the Christmas tree, turned to take a final look at it as I left the room, and proceeded upstairs to the bedroom. After the lights were out there and a quick round of Walton-like good nights we all drifted off to sleep.

The next morning I was the first one up. The unwritten rule at our house is that the first one awake in the morning makes the morning coffee. So, I eased out of bed and recoiled just slightly as my warm feet came in contact with the cold hardwood floor of the bedroom. "Slippers," I thought to myself and quickly slid into the pair I had left next to the bed.

As I sauntered slowly down the stairway my mind was on coffee and the gift I had received the night before. I really didn't consider myself a fashion-expert, even when it came to fishing apparel. But, this hat was quite classy and I was already fantasizing about the reception it would get when my fishing partners saw it this spring. I decided I should probably make a side trip on my way to the kitchen to try it on one more time.

At the bottom of the stairs, I turned right into our living room and stopped dead in my tracks. There, lying under our Christmas tree was Susie. Between her front paws I could make out a crumpled, wet brown mound. What the item was registered almost immediately with me. It was my new hat, or what remained of it.

Dogs can be very perceptive. Susie, in this case, realized something was wrong. It may have been my body language, the way my eyes locked with hers, or perhaps the blood-chilling scream that spewed from my mouth, I don't know which. Whatever the case, Susie exploded into motion and vacated the room, scattering gifts, bits of ribbon and paper in her wake.

Slowly I approached the sodden mass that lay under the tree. Disbelief, anger and sorrow raced through me. I had thoughts of what a hat made out of beagle hide would look like, but I shook that aside.

I quietly knelt down and picked up the remains of what I had thought would be a new companion to share the adventures of my future trips. Cradling the heap of wet felt in my arms, I stood up and turned to find my daughters and wife in the doorway watching me. The commotion in the living room had roused the rest of the family.

"What happ...," they began to ask but then fell silent as their eyes focused on what I was holding. There was a brief moment of silence as their eyes darted from me to the floor and then to one another. Simultaneously they broke out into smiles and laughter as they beheld my expression and the material in my arms.

"It's not that funny," I said. "This hat is ruined. I'll strangle that dog if I can find her."

"Let me look at it," Shirley said as she wiped away tears of laughter. "It doesn't look too bad, I'm sure we can fix it. Just needs some reshaping. Calm down."

My family did help resurrect the hat and it didn't turn out too bad. There were only two places in the brim where it looked like large bites had been taken out.

"Tell people it's a new design. Maybe it's supposed to help with vision when casting."

"Yeah dad, or tell them a story. Make something up."

"Or, just tell them the truth."

All possibilities I thought, but a tough decision about which one to use. The design story would have to be proved to be believable. The truth would seem ridiculous and probably give my buddies too much ammunition for day-long harassment.

That spring, I wore my hat for the first trip to the Arrowhead. I put it on when we arrived at the access road to Moose Creek. There was a short pause in our preparation as we readied ourselves for the walk in. Neal was the first to speak.

"Nice hat."

"Yeah, it was a Christmas gift. Really feels good."

"What's with the brim?" Ryan asked.

"What do you mean?"

"Well, what happened to it?"

"Oh, you mean the bite marks?" I asked. "Well, let me tell you, this hat belonged to my uncle, you know the one who had the run-in with that big bear? Well, he was...."

"Wait, "Ryan said. "The hat looks okay. Let's go."

Unspoken Words

All of the places of our lives are sanctuaries; some of them just happen to have steeples. And all of the people in our lives are saints; it is just that some of them have day jobs and most will never have feast days named for them.
~ Robert Benson

I am entranced by the wonders of nature. When the water is still and the trees and sky are reflected perfectly it is difficult to tell where one ends and the other begins. The way tamaracks shimmer as the wind ruffles their branches can stop me in my tracks. Some of those moments are solitary; others are shared.

One early morning I sat in the door of our tent with my oldest daughter, then seven. The sun was coming up over the mountain lake we were camped beside. The lake was still inky black; the sunlight had not yet descended to its surface. Steam was rising off the surface leaving a low cloud of vapor just above the water. The ghost-like outline of two loons faded in and out of the haze, and occasionally their cry broke the morning stillness. Gina and I sat huddled together with a sleeping bag wrapped around our shoulders as we watched the new day being born. As we sat transfixed by the scene before us One word from Gina broke the silence, "Wow." We both knew what she meant. This poignant father-daughter moment came on the morning after a tearful time-out. After having been told numerous times that it was too dangerous to run and skip around the campsite barefoot, that hiking boots were a non-negotiable item of apparel, Gina chose to scamper around in stocking feet instead. That action resulted in fifteen minutes of thinking time for her, alone in our tent. In a way, I suppose that could be construed as a spiritual awakening of sorts.

Some might think of these moments as religious experiences. I, however, consider them to be more spiritual. The difference for me is that religion brings the connotation of ritual, tradition and structure with it, whereas being spiritual can be defined by me and only requires a state of mind. It has a mystical element to it. Spiritual events can happen any time, anywhere and can incorporate many of the same teachings and beliefs that an organized practice embraces. Both have a place, but they are not necessarily the same.

Becoming lost in the sensations that nature provides is a consistent part of my being now, but recognizing the spiritual side of nature didn't happen for me all at once. I do know exactly when I started to really think about it and began to realize there was a strength of mind that the natural world offered me.

It happened on a cool spring morning over forty years ago. Not a cloud blemished the robin's egg blue sky. The early sun was shining brightly through the classroom windows; the greenhouse effect bringing the heat inside to a level that made attention difficult. In an attempt to moderate the room temperature, the teacher had opened those large, institutional windows about an inch to allow the cooler air from the outside to mix with the stale air inside. This did help temper the classroom's heat, but it also allowed the sounds of the birds as well as that intoxicating fresh smell of spring to enter the room. The buds on the maple trees outside of the church window bulged as they swelled in preparation to open.

It was 9:00 a.m., Saturday, April 12, 1958, opening day of trout season in Minnesota. My best friend, Arvo was probably fishing the willow roots hole on Scanlon Creek right now. I, however, was in catechism class. It wasn't just the fishing. I felt as if the day was calling to me to be outside and to drink in its wonders, but I was stuck.

In my youth I spent every Saturday from September through the end of May, from 9:00 to 11:00, listening to Father Francis or Sister DePaul as they droned on with the catechism lesson for the day. On most Saturdays I was able to endure the two hours and even pay some attention to what was being said about God, religion, and right versus wrong. I blankly stared and tried to focus on my little blue Baltimore Catechism but my thoughts were not there. This Saturday morning, trout season opened at 10:00, and it would be at least two hours past the opener before I could be on the stream. By that time, Arvo would have cleaned out all the best holes on Scanlon Creek.

The night before I asked my father if it would be all right to leave catechism an hour early. I thought that I was offering a good compromise since I would be in class for the first hour. His answer was not what I wanted to hear.

"This is important. There are many things you need to know. You're going to be confirmed in a year. You'll have many years to fish."

I tried to negotiate with him. "Dad, how about if I give up trout fishing next year for Lent?" I offered. "That's forty days to pay back the few hours I'll miss."

"Trout season doesn't even open until after Lent," my father said. "Nice try."

I played my trump and had nothing left to offer. So, I was present in those classes, at least physically, during the first two months of spring. But, on those Saturdays, visions of brook trout and their secret hiding places overshadowed any thoughts I might have about saints or sins. Heaven was being free to walk along Scanlon Creek and fish for brookies; hell was sitting through two hours of lessons before I could wet a line.

To the adults around me, it was important that I develop a religious base in my life. It was a natural step in a person's development and was traditionally handed down through families and the generations. The belief was that the family helped reinforce religious conviction with the aid of the church as the delivery system. My family was no different, therefore I was subject to that mode of teaching; catechism on Saturdays, church on Sundays and every religious holiday.

But, there were things I questioned about this belief system that I never could get answers to. Many of my friends did not attend church regularly, if at all, yet they seemed to be doing all right. They had good days and bad days, just as I did. Some of them were stellar students in school, some were like me. It just seemed to me that by sitting in church on Sunday morning for an hour and a half, or by attending two hours of catechism class every Saturday, I wasn't coming out any better than they were. As a matter of fact, it appeared to me that I was missing a lot.

I continued to be a part of this religious community, although increasingly mentally detached, until I turned eighteen. Coming to the age of majority during my senior year in high school meant that I was emancipated from the rules that governed children. As an adult I needed to register for the selective service, I had to look ahead to school or work and I could decide for myself what path my religious life would take.

Fortunately for me I had some positive mentors cross my path during that year, my great grandfather Albert Erickson being the one who furthered my questions about spirituality and religion. He was a large man but very soft-spoken. Born in 1882, he had stories and experiences to share that kept my brother and me transfixed and gap-mouthed at his feet. He and I never directly talked about religious dogma, but on occasion he might share a belief or principle that he held to be true. Many of these did not align with the teachings with which I was raised.

He went to church regularly, but wasn't a regular at any particular church. On Sundays, he would attend whichever congregation happened to be near where he was that day. His feeling was that it didn't matter what building you were in or if you were even in a building, it just mattered that you took time. To him there was sanctity in wandering through his lumber mill and stopping to savor the aroma of fresh cut cedar or pine.

"There's no Hell that bad people go to after they die," he once said. "We are all living in Hell right now. When we finish our mission here and die, we all go on to a better place."

I asked if he meant heaven.

"Could be," he said, "or it could just be a better place. Depends on the life you've lived."

His words didn't do much to comfort me. What they did was continue to fuel the questioning that I had about organized religion. I wanted answers, but they just wouldn't come. I was told to trust and just believe, but there were too many uncertainties for me to merely brush aside. I continued to search for meaning into my early twenties, never finding an answer, just becoming more perplexed. I was brought up and confirmed in the Catholic Church but began to look at other religious groups as I grew older.

I spent some time with a fundamentalist gospel group but found that to be too intense and narrow for my liking. For a time I dropped away from any formal religion at all. I continued along that path during my college years, really not giving much thought or concern for the religious world. I felt content and was getting my spiritual needs met through life experiences, although I didn't realize it at the time.

Then, after college I joined a Methodist Church. For a time it seemed that it was the spiritual place that I had been looking for. That is, until one spring Sunday I was sitting in a pew, half-listening to the sermon but thinking about being where I was. I asked myself, "Why am I here in church?" The only answer I could give myself was that I was there because the person with me needed a ride. That was the last Sunday I spent in that church.

Some people believe everything happens for a reason while others hold to the tenet that all things are random and you make out of them what you want. Whichever it is, a few months later I had an experience that helped me focus.

I traveled to Glacier National Park that summer. I had heard of the majesty of the Rocky Mountains but the description truly paled next to actually being there. I set up camp in St. Mary, Montana and made day excursions from there. Part of the time I spent going to the popular tourist sites which were indeed amazing. Other times I struck out on my own. I spent a day being lost along a crystal clear creek. Another time I hiked into a hidden mountain lake. The lake was green at the surface but continued to deepen in blue-green as the water got deeper. As I looked down at it, the lake appeared to have no bottom.

One day I walked across alpine snowfields and on another I stood next to mountain goats as they lay in the mountain snow to cool off. I drank water out of a stream that was so cold it hurt my teeth. As I sat outside my tent at night I witnessed stars so bright they actually cast shadows across the ground. During those days and nights I recognized the feelings I struggled with years ago in catechism class. But it wasn't until the drive home to Minnesota that things made sense to me. Ironically thanks to a popular singer of the time.

Somewhere between Montana and North Dakota I heard a song on my car radio and its words struck me like a hammer. As a youngster I probably would have hummed along or moved to the beat of the song, not really hearing the lyrics but age had made me more introspective. John Denver began to sing about a person being born in the summer of his twenty-seventh year. I slowed the car as I heard him sing about going home to a place he's never been before.

For me, that moment was one of those life epiphanies that I believe we all have. I was in the right frame of mind just coming back from my first trip to the Rocky Mountains. I was still riding along in a state of euphoria from my experience and I happened to be twenty-seven. I pulled the car to the shoulder of the road, listened to John finish his song and realized the song was not only about the mountains, he was singing about the feelings that nature evokes in me. He was singing about the quiet, inner peace brought on by those moments.

Later, during my drive home I realized that I didn't have to search for meaning or answers anymore; they were right in front of me all the time. It was the old look AND see rule but I had not been using it. However, now I try to remember how important that tenet is and attempt to utilize it in most things I do.

Recently as I was snow shoeing along McCarty Creek with two close friends this belief was reinforced for me again. It was one of those weather perfect days that sometimes happen in February; a day when Mother Nature tries to trick you into believing winter is over.

The temperature had risen to the mid twenties and we had shed our jackets in favor of sweaters and long-sleeved t-shirts. There were no clouds in the sky to block a blue color that comes close to what sapphire must be. The snow's whiteness would have been blinding if not for our tinted glasses. The air was fresh but did not have the biting crispness of subzero days and you could actually feel each breath fill not just your lungs but your entire being. The only breaks in the surface of the waist-deep snow were occasional animal tracks. One set in particular drew our attention. The long indentation looked as if it had been made by someone dragging a log or something through the snow. But after looking into the trough we could see the side by side tracks that an otter had made as it slithered and bounded through the snow.

As the three of us plodded along, the swish and crunch of our snowshoes was the only sound to break the stillness. No breeze or winter bird stirred the air. Later, reminiscing about that walk, the three of us agreed that we had been completely immersed in the experience and our surroundings. Though words weren't spoken, there was a common communication among us.

I had not visited this area in over thirty years, but I remembered the landscape as if I had been back only yesterday. Looking around I recognized the rise in elevation ahead of us that bordered the old homestead clearing and the beginning of the meadows. We climbed the backside of that rise and walked through the jack pines that crowned the top. From that hill, the meadows and large pool below where the settlers had built their home came into view. The familiar sight triggered thoughts of trips to this spot that I had made with an old friend, Neal. I felt a oneness with nature, an inner peace that filled me to my soul.

As my two friends stood on that hilltop looking out over the meadow above McCarty Creek, it occurred to me that this moment needed to be shared. I reached into my jacket pocket, pulled out my cell phone and called Neal. The phone rang a few times, there was an audible click and then "Hello?"

"Neal, this is Rudy."

"Yeah, what's up?"

" It's a bright sunny day. The snow is waist deep and the temp is in the twenties. I'm standing on the hill above the old homestead on the McCarty."

There was a pause on his end and then he said what I had been feeling.

"I'm right with you, buddy."

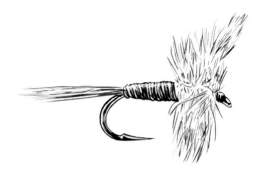

List of Illustrations

Rudy's Glossary

Terms defined by their use in the Arrowhead.

Alder
A low growing shrub sometimes called Tag Alder that can be found along streams and in low wet areas. Its branches grow thickly and intertwine.

Arrowhead
A region of northern Minnesota that juts into Lake Superior named for its arrowhead shape.

Balm of Gilead
A tree that looks similar to a poplar tree. It has shiny leaves and exudes a sticky residue with a sweet and pungent odor in the spring. Not of much value for logging or for firewood.

Beaver pond
The body of water held behind a beaver dam.

Brookie
Slang term for Eastern Brook Trout

Browns or Brown	Slang term for German Brown Trout
BWCA	Boundary Waters Canoe Area, a designated wilderness area on the Minnesota/Canadian border.
Cloquet	A small paper mill town in northern Minnesota.
Crawlers	Slang term for night crawlers. Large worms used as bait.
Creel	A small wicker basket mainly used by anglers to hold fish. Designed to function as an evaporative cooler when lined with moss and dipped into the creek to keep the catch chilled. Caught fish are inserted through a slot in the top held in place by a small leather strap.
Crooked Lake	The base camp for our trips owned and operated by the Schumachers.
Culvert	A metal, tube-like structure used to help drainage around and under roads.
Dead Fall	Type of animal trap which uses a large, heavy object to kill the animals by falling on it.
Deadfish Lake	A small, boggy lake popular with duck hunters west of Cloquet, Minnesota.

Deadwaters	Slow deep water above the beginning of the drainage to a lake or watershed.
Ditchbanks	Local name for a popular area for hunters consisting of old drainage ditches near Cloquet, Minnesota.
Dogwood	A short shrub that grows along most logging roads. Its bark is green in the summer and turns bright red in the fall and winter.
Escarpment	The rise in the land primarily composed of basalt and granite from the shores of Lake Superior to the inland plateau which was originally the ancient shore of Lake Superior.
Esker	A long narrow deposit of coarse gravel forming a ridge-like landscape that is the result of glacial activity.
Feeder brook	A small brook or stream that enters a larger stream and often its water source.
Finland	A very small community in northern Minnesota.
Floating bog	Vegetation that has grown out and floats on the water surface. The roots of the plants intertwine to form a rug-like, suspended surface.
Game Trail	Moose, deer, and other wildlife walk these trails regularly and leave fairly clear paths through the forest.

Grade	Slang for a rail bed or road.
Hellgrammites	Aquatic insects that are a favorite food of trout.
Holes	A slang term for the places most likely to hold fish in a stream.
Honey Hole	The best fishing spot on a stream.
International Scout	A Four-wheel drive vehicle made by International Harvester Company much like the Jeep Cherokee.
Isabella	A very small northern Minnesota community.
Labrador tea	A very low shrub that grows along the stream banks. Usually found in very wet areas. The leaves were dried and used as tea by the French Voyageurs.
Lassie	Popular TV show from the 1950's about a collie and her master.
Logging camp	Places where the lumberjacks lived while working in the woods.
Log landing	A place designated for trains or trucks to pick up cut logs. Also referred to as a saw landing or landing.
Lunker	A large fish, bigger than the average size associated with that species.

Meadow(s)	The open area left treeless after a beaver dam has flooded. From a distance a meadow looks like an open field. Usually used as a plural.
Mepps	A fishing lure company located in Antigo, Wisconsin.
Moraine	Gravel deposits left behind across Minnesota and Wisconsin by glaciers.
Muddler	A fly pattern that is supposed to mimic a minnow or sculpin.
Narrows	A place where a river becomes constricted often between pools of water.
Northshore	An area along the northwest coast of Lake Superior between Duluth, Minnesota and the Canadian border.
Nymphs	Collective term for immature aquatic insects and a favorite food for trout. It is also a wet fly pattern.
Railbed	The surface a railroad is built on (commonly made of crushed coarse stone).
Rin-Tin-Tin`	Popular TV show from the 1950s about a young boy and his dog who lived on a military fort in the 1800's.
Sculpin	A small minnow trout feed on.

Slabs	Side pieces of wood cut off of a log during the sawing process, usually discarded at the sawing site.
Spring hole	A deep hole made by a spring as it bubbles out of the ground.
Steelheads	Term used for the rainbow trout that migrate from Lake Superior in the spring.
Topo	Slang term for topographic map.
Tote Road	Synonym for logging road.
Trestle Inn	A great local watering hole and eatery located along Cramer Road .
Twelve incher	A trout twelve inches in length (brook trout are referred to by their length).
Whitethroats	White Fronted Sparrows that inhabit the marshy areas around the trout streams.
Whyte	At one time 250 people lived in this logging stop near the Alger Smith Line, now it is a crossroads in the forest.
Winter road	A road used for logging during winter months. It traverses wet low land and can support the heavy machinery only after the ground freezes.

Wooly Bugger   A large, usually black or dark colored wet fly.

Zebco   Fishing equipment manufacturer originally the Zero Hour Bomb Company located in Tulsa, Oklahoma. They began manufacturing fishing reels in 1949.

About the Author

Rudy "Rick" Senarighi was born and raised in Cloquet, Minnesota. He attended the University of Minnesota at Duluth and graduated in 1969. He began trout fishing as a youngster in Minnesota, often riding his bicycle eight miles in the dark to be on the stream by sunrise. This passion continues today. Writing a book about his experiences trout fishing in northern Minnesota was a dream he nurtured for many years. Rudy taught junior high school in Superior, Wisconsin for seven years before returning to school for graduate work in Educational Psychology. He moved to Door County, Wisconsin and was employed by the Sturgeon Bay Schools for 25 years as their middle school guidance counselor. A diagnosis of cancer in early 2000 prompted him to reassess his life's priorities and begin cataloging his stories. In January of 2003, he retired from his work in schools and has since volunteered nationwide teaching young people leadership skills and a love of the outdoors. Rudy currently does educational training and consulting work in Wisconsin. When he is not fishing or writing he can be found gardening, running, and traveling the world with his wife Shirley and daughters Gina and Angie.

All profits from the sale of his books are donated to the American Cancer Society.